What Readers Are Saying

We all need a friend who sits with us in the hard, and, when the time is right, speaks the truth of God's love and care over us. In *Something Good Will Grow*, Nicole not only meets you where you are, but she uplifts and equips you with the tools you need to walk with the Lord through the darkness and into the light. She also does a beautiful job of acknowledging what is not fun about suffering, while encouraging us to fix our eyes squarely on Jesus and to live expectantly, trusting in God's goodness. – Carrie K.

Nicole Jacobsmeyer boldly shares her life—the good, the bad, and the broken—in a way that is gospel-centered. *Something Good Will Grow* invited me to see my suffering through a heavenly lens, focusing on God above all. Her transparency is refreshing and her unashamed proclamation of Jesus Christ is unceasingly good, even in the most dire of circumstances. This book is a much-needed invitation to refocus my perspective. – Anna W.

Something Good Will Grow came into my life at exactly the right time. During a season where I've been trying to reconnect and strengthen my faith, this book gently reminded me to release my worries to God and trust Him more fully. It encouraged me to slow down, be still, and allow Him to work through my pain and struggles rather than trying to carry everything alone. One of the most meaningful messages was the reminder that our suffering is not without purpose when we surrender it to Him. This book left me feeling comforted, hopeful, and reminded that even through difficult seasons, something good truly can grow. – Christina S.

Something Good Will Grow offers a compelling reminder that even the deepest seasons of suffering are never wasted in the hands of our good and gracious God. Nicole points readers beyond temporary, unsatisfactory relief to the lasting treasure of knowing Jesus more intimately with honesty, wisdom, and unwavering biblical truth. Each chapter beautifully and powerfully communicates how pain and suffering can become the very place where faith is refined, and Christ becomes more precious than ever before. This is a convicting, encouraging, and hope-filled resource for anyone longing to find purpose, endurance, and deeper fellowship with Christ in the midst of any trial. – Kelsey W.

Nicole has created a lifeline for those seeking a meaningful understanding of their faith in Christ. Her personal testimony and use of Scripture create a powerful connection that is easy to understand and, most importantly, relatable. Encouraging and uplifting, *Something Good Will Grow* reminds us that we are never alone when God comes first. This book will renew and strengthen your foundation in Christ. – Bethany D.

Something Good Will Grow

Finding God's Heart in the Soil of Suffering

NICOLE JACOBSMEYER

MOODY PUBLISHERS
CHICAGO

All emphasis to Scripture has been added.

Edited by Pamela Joy Pugh
Interior design: Brandi Davis
Cover design: Brittany Schrock
Cover image: Cover image of flowers copyright © 2026 by Odua Images/Adobe Stock (25766863). All rights reserved.

Library of Congress Cataloging-in-Publication Data

Names: Jacobsmeyer, Nicole author
Title: Something good will grow : finding God's heart in the soil of suffering / Nicole Jacobsmeyer.
Description: Chicago : Moody Publishers, [2026] | Includes bibliographical references. | Summary: "This book helps you place your pain in God's hands, equips you to persevere, and gives you a fresh vision to remain faithful. God wants to bring forth something beautiful-something good-from your suffering. Don't miss it. Even here, you can become radiant in and to a hurting world"-- Provided by publisher.
Identifiers: LCCN 2026022187 (print) | LCCN 2026022188 (ebook) | ISBN 9780802438065 paperback | ISBN 9780802468024 ebook
Subjects: LCSH: Suffering--Religious aspects--Christianity | Consolation
Classification: LCC BV4909 .J255 2026 (print) | LCC BV4909 (ebook)
LC record available at https://lccn.loc.gov/2026022187
LC ebook record available at https://lccn.loc.gov/2026022188

Originally delivered by fleets of horse-drawn wagons, the affordable paperbacks from D. L. Moody's publishing house resourced the church and served everyday people. Now, after more than 125 years of publishing and ministry, Moody Publishers' mission remains the same—even if our delivery systems have changed a bit. For more information on other books (and resources) created from a biblical perspective, go to www.moodypublishers.com or write to:

Moody Publishers
820 N. LaSalle Boulevard
Chicago, IL 60610

1 3 5 7 9 10 8 6 4 2

Printed in the United States of America

To my beautiful daughter, Madison.

May you always see the faithful and loving hand of God in your life.

Contents

Dear Reader,

These pages hold painful pieces of my story, but more than that, they bear witness to the unwavering character and faithfulness of God. While this book speaks honestly about seasons of deep suffering, including the mention of sexual assault, it does not recount the details of that experience.

If you have experienced this injustice, I want you to know before you turn the page that rape is mentioned in this book. But praise God darkness does not have the final word in our lives.

My prayer is that you will see God's faithfulness in your story and find hope in Him through every page.

Nicole

Blooming in the Dark

And after you have suffered a little while, the God of all grace, who has called you to his eternal glory in Christ, will himself restore, confirm, strengthen, and establish you.

1 PETER 5:10 ESV

I love New Year's Eve! I can count on one hand how many times I've made it to midnight, but there's just something sweet about spending time reflecting on all that God has done. He is always working, providing, and teaching, and the ending of every year reminds me of how great He is, was, and will always be.

Most years, I ask God to give me a word, verse, or topic to study in the upcoming season. Maybe you do the same. I love to look back on the words and verses God has given me over time and see how His faithfulness and goodness permeate every year, even those filled with heartache.

A few years back, the word the Lord impressed on my heart was *bloom*.

Bloom

I had just come off a few extremely difficult years that included a cancer diagnosis, severe depression, our family's move across the country, and a miscarriage. I was thrilled with the word *bloom* because it sounded so hopeful, so . . . encouraging. I felt a breath of fresh air after getting the wind knocked out of me. *This year will be good,* I thought.

In the back of my mind, I anticipated that God must be up to something big and prosperous and maybe even extravagant in my life. When I thought of *bloom*, I thought of growth and vibrant color developing into something even more beautiful. I began to imagine something showy and worthy of being seen and appreciated. I daydreamed about finally seeing the fruits of all my hard work.

I must have heard the Lord wrong. Maybe He really meant doom or gloom and I just got the letters mixed up.

But what I slowly started to learn as the year progressed was that my *blooming* looked a lot like closed doors. It was a year of weeping at night over so many disappointments that I lost track of what was causing my pain. Instead of prosperity, my *blooming* looked a lot like humility, brokenness, and walking in obedience and faithfulness in the dark when no one was watching or applauding. It was an extremely lonely season and I felt completely forgotten by God and others.

I began to ask, "Why did God give me such an encouraging word only to have me live out the opposite?" I was withering away, fading behind the what-could-have-beens, the misunderstandings, the physical setbacks, and the insecurities that reared their ugly head. It was becoming a year of stress and false hope. I felt so . . . unseen. More than that, I was angry. *I must have heard the Lord wrong. Maybe He really meant doom or gloom and I just got the letters mixed up.* Or maybe I was basing the word on my own emotions, hearing what I *wanted* to hear, something hopeful, after so much suffering the years prior.

But looking back, here is what I know to be true: "His ways are not our ways and His thoughts are not our thoughts" (Isa. 55:8–9). They are so much better! I didn't misunderstand. *Bloom* really was my word.

The Lord woke me up early one morning toward the middle of that year and I felt a prompting to look up "flowers that bloom at night." I'm not much of a gardener and am definitely not blessed with a green thumb. I didn't think it was even possible for flowers to bloom at night. But I thought, *why not check?*

I rolled over, trying not to wake my husband, grabbed my glasses, and reached for my phone. As I squinted my eyes and adjusted to the light, what I found was absolutely beautiful.

What blooms at night? Flowers! (At least some of them.) Did you know this? These night flowers bloom in the dark, in the colder temperatures, and when no one is watching. They are *extravagant* and some of the most fragrant of all the flowers God has created. Some even have the brightest white coloring, reflecting the moon, and glowing throughout the garden while illuminating everything around them. Breathtaking!

When I read this, it all clicked. Before learning about these night-blooming flowers, I had equated blooming with blessings, favor, and good things. Over time, I found that the blessing was actually in the growth that happens beneath the surface, behind the scenes, and when no one else notices. The blessing was in my spiritual development in the hard and holy places of darkness when no one else was there but the Lord. It was in the cold and uncomfortable temperatures of quietness, conviction, and forgiveness that I was, in fact, blooming.

> I had equated blooming with good things, but I found that the blessing was in the growth that happened beneath the surface.

Night Flowers

I understand that you may have a vast and looming darkness in your life right now that feels unending and hopeless and lonely, but let's not mistake it for God's wrath or displeasure. He is doing a good work in your life that will bring Him glory. Just as the sun rises in the morning, there will be a sunset that eventually ends with a pitch-black sky, complete darkness until early the next morning, when hope and light come again. We all have something that grieves our spirits, hidden battles that maybe only few know of, and we're all up against evil and trials we can't run from. But we each have the opportunity to be night flowers, fed all day by the Son and blooming in the dark for His glory.

Each trial in our lives is a crossroads in our faith, and we have the opportunity to choose: Will we surrender in our brokenness and learn to suffer well? Or will we miss out on the most beautiful, abundant, and sanctifying work of our faith that suffering ushers in?

Believe He will do exceedingly and abundantly more in your life. Believe He will restore, redeem, and strengthen you.

Suffering well is not for the faint of heart. The narrow road to bringing God glory is one of self-denial, enduring hardships with hope, and understanding the peace of being under His perfect authority and will, not our own. God uses our suffering to form us into the most fragrant and brightest white flower, reflecting the light of Christ to the entire garden. What the Lord offers us is far better, deeper, and more lasting than any quick fix or promise that the world offers.

Believe He will do exceedingly and abundantly more in your life. Believe He will restore, redeem, and strengthen you. That is my goal as you read the pages to come, that you will believe and hope and smile and dance again. Not because your outcome was perfect or exactly what you thought it would look like, but because you finally realized that you were never alone. God was there the entire time in the heartache of the night as your greatest hope and strength.

If you're ready for the difficult but life-changing truth of what blooming really looks like as a disciple of Christ, this book is for you. Let's walk this journey together.

Blooming in the Dark

Something Good to Remember: We each have the opportunity to be night flowers, fed all day by the Son and blooming in the dark for His glory.

For Reflection: In what way(s) are you confident that God is growing something good in your life through pain? If you're not sure He is, are you open to the idea?

For Meditation: Romans 5:3–5

To Pray: *God, I believe You are always restoring, redeeming, and strengthening me. Even when it looks like there's no hope and my suffering feels unending, thank You for producing in me the endurance to keep going and the grace to get through. I love You so much. Amen.*

chapter 1

When Life Is More Than You Can Handle: Abundance in Christ

And my God will supply every need of yours according to his riches in glory in Christ Jesus.

PHILIPPIANS 4:19 ESV

Something Good Will Grow

When life overwhelms, His abundant grace overwhelms us all the more.

One of my favorite things to do on our farm is take our dog, Bear, for walks around our property. I cry. I talk. I sweat. I ask questions. I raise my voice on occasion. The neighbors' horses in the pasture, the birds gliding from tree to tree, the occasional deer, squirrel, or bunny, and our cows, chickens, and dogs are the only ones that listen in as I clear my head and talk with God.

I vividly remember one beautiful, chilly November morning. The unwelcomed Southern heat and humidity (that I still haven't yet quite adjusted to) had slowly crept into October, so I was beyond grateful for the cold. I was on my walk, wrestling with this idea of continuing to be given more than I can handle in life. I'd already walked through my fair share of pain, so I wondered out loud, "Can I be done with pain now? Can I turn in my badge of suffering yet?"

As my feet pounded the dirt and my heart pounded in my chest, I realized that God is allowing me to face more than I can handle. Allowing. I would soon understand that the more pain that came my way, the more of His abundant grace I would experience.

When God Overwhelms with Grace

I had just had a procedure to remove a precancerous lesion on my back. I was still getting over a nasty head cold, likely because I barely have any lymph nodes left in my neck from a prior surgery (more on this later), I hadn't slept much due to my husband's work schedule, and I was exhausted from the daily grind of homeschooling and motherhood. There was nothing particularly awful or tragic that I was facing at the moment; no major trials as I had in the past. Just a lot of "little" sufferings all at once that made me feel like I was dealing with more than I could handle. I desperately wanted to find perspective, but couldn't see God in any of it.

Have you been there? Maybe your life is filled with worst-case scenarios right now. (If that's the case, I pray this book landed in your hands at just the right moment.) Or maybe your life is just life, sprinkled with pain. Whether I have a traumatic event, a great loss, deep sorrows, or just a week full of low moments like this one, more than ever I am beginning to crave different answers to my aching questions about suffering. Over time I have found myself shifting my hidden questions to God concerning suffering from, *Why is this happening?* or *Why did You allow this?* to *Help me see You in my pain, Lord!* and *What can I learn from You in this?*

My questions for God once stemmed from selfishness and understandable anger. Now, they are meek and humble prayers when life overwhelms. I spent over a decade of my life wondering why evil was happening to me, why God allowed pain, and why He didn't save me or rescue me in the way that I thought was best. Now I'm in a season of surrendering in my suffering and seeing the peace that comes when our hope is truly in Jesus. But it didn't come easy.

When I have more than I can handle or when life overwhelms, I want to know that what I'm walking through won't be wasted. I want to allow God to guide me. You have the same desire, don't you? We all do. We want to know that all this pain and suffering we experience has *meaning*. If we don't see a purpose, we become hopeless and feel like we can't endure.

For that reason, I think it's important to recognize that sometimes we walk through difficult things just because we live in a fallen world. Maybe you twisted your ankle while walking down the stairs (this just happened to me), had an argument with your spouse, left your grocery list at home, or forgot to pay the electricity bill. That doesn't mean that Satan is always responsible. If we're being honest, sometimes we're the cause of our own sufferings (like when I chose to carry way too much laundry and missed a step because I couldn't see over the towels). Let's not fall into the trap of over-spiritualizing everyday life.

> Everything we walk through is an opportunity to increase our dependence on God.

But everything we walk through—whether small or big and no matter the cause, hard things that affect our health, our family, our relationships, our finances, or our beliefs—each one is an opportunity to increase our dependence on God. He wants to reveal His heart to us in the hard things. It becomes less about learning how great we can become because of painful times, and more about remembering how great God already is in these difficulties. It's about the hope we have on this side of eternity when everything around us seems hopeless. It's about how He grows us, even though we are undeserving and don't see any purpose right away. Every heartache points back to Him and our dependence on Him. What abundant grace!

Sometimes God fixes things immediately in our lives and we see miraculous works before our very own eyes. But most of the time, the pain in our lives reveals things we need to work on, issues that need to be confronted, idols we need to ditch, people we need to forgive, conversations that need to happen, sin that needs to be exposed, continued healing that needs to be addressed, boundaries that need to be set, control that needs to be released, and things about the Lord that we need to comprehend.

Truthfully, there is always something to learn but the desire to even want to learn can get lost behind the raw emotions we are presently experiencing. So before we learn "all the things," if we could just remember that pain is an opportunity to become more like Christ, we can at least have an ounce of hope in the worst of circumstances

Pain also gives us the opportunity to see that when life overwhelms, His abundant grace overwhelms us all the more. The ultimate prize that develops out of pain and suffering is a more intimate knowledge of Jesus Himself.

The Truth about Suffering

It's popular—and incorrect—to say God will never give us more than we can handle, and to "prove" this, many quote 1 Corinthians 10:12–13: "If you think you are standing strong, be careful not to fall. The temptations in your life are no different from what others experience. And God is faithful. He will not allow the temptation to be more than you can stand. When you are tempted, he will show you a way out so that you can endure."

Many believe that God is saying He'll never allow more *sorrow* than we have the strength to endure. But if you read that whole chapter, you'll see that it's a warning for the Christian who is fighting against the temptation of *idolatry*, or desiring wrong things that are contrary to God's way. If we have temptation, there is a way out because with Christ, we have the Holy Spirit to guide us and help us endure the enticements of this world. He won't let us be tempted beyond what we can endure.

Of course, God *will* give us more than we can handle; otherwise, we would not need to depend on Him.

As Christians, we are told that we will suffer with and for Christ (Rom. 8:17). This means that, like Christ, we are called to deny ourselves and take up our cross by living a life of humble surrender to the Father. Our life is no longer our own. The apostle John quotes Jesus, who tells us we will all have trials and sorrows (John 16:33). The thought that we would *not* be given more than we can handle in life is in no way represented in 1 Corinthians 10 or in any other place in the Word of God.

What else is it supposed to mean when we have trials by fire (1 Peter 1:7)? What's the fire? More than we can deal with. Hardships. Consuming pain. Christ went to the cross, endured the excruciating suffering and held the sin, shame, and grief of the entire world, past, present, and future. What was His reward? Glorifying the Father by sacrificing Himself and saving mankind. We the redeemed are His reward. If we are supposed to share in Christ's sufferings, we will also have pain but, as Christ experienced, our reward is great.

> His purpose is not to bring you pain, but God allows your pain to grow you and develop you, and He never ceases to be good, kind, and sovereign.

However, we often choose not to believe this out of our own pride and comfort. We tell ourselves, *we can handle life on our own. We can get through anything in our own strength. God is too nice to allow hard things for the faithful Christian.* These are false proclamations that we like to declare as truth. We live in a fallen world, full of evil, sin, and free will, and we are all sinners in desperate need of a Savior. God is faithful, kind, and loyal, while permitting trials to come. We can be confident that everything is under His authority (1 Cor. 15:27).

His purpose is not to bring you pain, but God allows your pain to grow you and develop you, and He never ceases to be good, kind, and sovereign.

Again, John 16:33 (ESV) says, "I have said these things to you, that in me you may have peace. In the world you will have tribulation. But take heart; I have overcome the world." In 2 Timothy 3:12 (ESV), the apostle Paul writes, "All who desire to live a godly life in Christ Jesus will be persecuted." Knowing these Scriptures is one thing. Living them out is an entirely different story, let alone living them out well.

Have I been given more than I can handle in certain seasons of life? You bet. Have you? Absolutely. Yes, we will have unthinkable pain, but His love and grace through it all is undeniable. His strength replaces the weakness that abounds in our life. *When our life overwhelms, His abundant goodness overwhelms us all the more.*

"Let It Be to Me"

What is this abundant goodness we talk about? How does it work?

A beautiful biblical example of this abundant way of life is Jesus' mother, Mary. Mary was a young woman, obedient through surrender; she was willing and full of directed purpose. We talk about her a lot in our faith because it can benefit us to consider how this young woman would be so honored to do as God asked through circumstances any stranger would look down upon. Pregnant before marriage? It was seen as dishonoring to her family and her culture and even to God.

But then God did the impossible and made something that appeared dishonorable into the most honored role a woman could have: carrying the Son of God

While we don't know much about Mary's life before pregnancy, she fully received what the Lord had to offer. *She was open and willing.*

Luke 1 describes the angel Gabriel coming to Mary. He said, "Greetings O favored one, the Lord is with you!" After hearing the message the angel brought, she responded with, "Behold I am the servant of the Lord; let it be to me according to your word" (vv. 28, 38 ESV). Mary called herself a servant of the Lord first and foremost. She didn't argue with God's grand plan to send His Son as our Redeemer through her womb. Though supernatural, her pregnancy was most likely not the most enjoyable or painless experience. She traveled while pregnant, perhaps far from family. But when the time came, she gave birth to the Savior of the world and was able to forever play a huge role in the story of His kingdom. What abundance in Christ she experienced!

> When you surrender to Him when life is more than you can handle, you'll start to see Him through it all.

Do we live our lives like this? Do we truly say, "Lord, I am Your servant; let your will be done"? Because when we do, we can watch Him trade our pain for His abundance of grace and peace and love and provision.

Let this wash over you.

You may not see it or believe it, but I *know* when you surrender to Him when life is more than you can handle, you'll start to see Him through it all. The beautiful and mysterious exchange of us giving Him our pain, everything we lost, everything that was said, everything that was done, and then His giving us Himself in return is the greatest and most powerful gift! What a gracious God.

The Paradox of Abundance

I have experienced more than my fair share of pain. I'm sure you have, too. Sleepless nights of fear . . . depression and anxiety that leads to suicidal thoughts . . . losing someone and the grief that changes you . . . health challenges that debilitate you and relationships that break you . . . the struggle of forgiving those who show no remorse or repentance for their wicked ways . . . being devalued, feeling less than, violated, and spiritually abused.

The pain I've personally walked through includes cancer, rape, manipulation, miscarriage, devastating relational pain, depression, and loneliness. I have fought, I have lost, I have hurt, I have been shattered. I have questioned, I have doubted, I have wrestled, and I have been broken beyond my own repair.

And I understand the gravity of my own sin and desperate need for a Savior.

Because I understand seasons of life that are completely overwhelming, it's in those moments that I find myself asking the question, *How am I supposed to live an abundant life if I'm constantly given more than I can handle?* Have you ever thought that in the middle of a hardship?

Jesus said, "The thief comes only to steal and kill and destroy. I came that they may have life and have it abundantly!" (John 10:10 ESV). Life abundant! The chapter continues by Jesus explaining that He is the Good Shepherd who lays His life down for His sheep. I always read that passage and think, "Yes! Satan has nothing on me! I have abundance in Christ!"

Abundance in my Christian walk means more of Christ and less of me; it's life to the fullest in Him, with Him, no matter the cost. When we are lacking and weak and just offer Him whatever small part of ourselves is left, He graciously lavishes His love and blessing on us. His love is incomprehensible to our human understanding.

When we have nothing, He has everything.

When we are weak, He is strong.

When we have more than we can handle, He pours out more undeserved grace.

Christianity is full of paradoxes that can make no sense in our human minds yet often bring us the most sense of reassurance in our troubles. These key truths are a dichotomy of ideas that don't seem to go together.

> To live is Christ, to die is gain. (Phil. 1:21)
>
> We are sinners but sanctified saints. (Rom. 3:23–24)
>
> We are sinned against but forgive. (Col. 3:13)
>
> We have enemies but pray for them. (Matt. 5:44)
>
> The first shall be last. (Matt. 20:16)
>
> We suffer and also rejoice. (Rom. 5:3–5)

How can we conceptualize this way of living as finite humans when we are surrounded by the world's call to only serve ourselves? How does one relish His abundance when the world around us is spinning in chaos and utter depravity? Here are a few reminders I pray will be a balm of encouragement from one hurting sister to another.

How to have Christ's abundance when we have a plethora of pain:

Receive

When I go to coffee with a new friend and she pays for me, I get weird. I wonder, *Does she think I'm poor? Does she want to butter me up for what she's going to say? Will our friendship be ruined if I forget to buy her coffee next time?* I know, that's overthinking. Some of us are just better at receiving than others, but can I encourage you to open yourself up to receiving Christ's abundant grace in your life?

In the most overwhelming of seasons, we must exchange our lack of understanding for His great grace and wisdom. We must be open to receiving what He has to offer in a time when it feels that the world has stripped us of everything we once had that was good and beautiful. We must be willing to open our palms to the Lord, in surrender and sacrifice, and receive from the only One who can pour into us. What He offers us in our weakness is truly the only thing worth receiving.

Focus

We live in an all-consuming, information overload, instant gratification world with social media constantly at our fingertips. It's not good for us. We were not meant to be pulled in a million different directions, seeking approval and trying to outperform the next person. We need to go back to a one-track mind. We must not deviate from the narrow road. One of the biggest lies and tendencies we have is to run, to change course, to fill our own voids, to squander what we have, to trust only ourselves. When things are overwhelming, we must focus and stay the course. We do this by reading the Word, listening to sound theology, having accountability and praying for strength to get through, and living in the boundaries of His grace and discipline from the things that are not good for our souls. Let God replace all of the worldly attractions with His wonderful abundance and refocus your heart to what truly matters in this life.

Invite

It's easy to feel ashamed or like you're "too much" when you have so much pain. I was talking with a friend the other day who shared that her kids were sick, mold from water damage had just been discovered throughout her house and, to top it all off, she lost her job. When she apologized because she felt like a "bad friend" for being in a season of need and slow communication, I assured her that her circumstances in no way defined our friendship.

It's through the hardships that our faith grows, and because of that we can have hope in this season we're in.

This is how it needs to be with the Lord. We don't need to be ashamed to come to the Father with our pain and desires and needs and tears. Invite the Lord first, and then others into your pain. We are not meant to live alone or endure alone. Let people in. Invite those trusted people into your life. We put pressure on ourselves to be everything to everyone, but may I give you permission today to not be so strong? This is your time to lean on others and let them help with empathy, a listening ear, practical needs, and the assurance of their prayers.

Earthly abundance in the way we humanly think (e.g., conflict-free marriage, healthy children, a balanced home and work life, lots of friends, living in perfect peace, never anxious or wanting more) will not push us to Christ like trials will. It's through the hardships that our faith grows, and because of that we can have hope in this season we're in. God in His great love for us won't leave us on the ground in despair, but He will make something beautiful again in our life. More than that, His abundance and goodness give us the hope to keep going. Seek Him first. Receive what He wants to offer you in this season, stay the course and invite people in.

Truth to Write

Let's allow the Word to wash over us before moving to the next chapter. Take a moment to write out the passages listed, asking the Lord to sear them into your heart.

Philippians 4:19
2 Corinthians 1:5
2 Corinthians 9:8

I understand praying "Lord, come quickly" or wishing the days away because the pain you are walking through is too much and unbearable. I know we have a hard time grasping His faithfulness until hardships have resolved. I know we see the good after the fact, but what I pray is that we get better at seeing Him *during* the trial and recognizing His abundant love and feeling His presence in the middle of the pain.

Today, as I go on another prayer walk around the farm, I'm praying that your overwhelming pain turns to recognizing the overwhelming blessing, grace, and abundance that are ours in Jesus. I also pray that as we work this concept out together in the pages to come, we will know without a doubt that He is close, that He loves us, and that He will grow something good in our lives even when we have more than we can handle.

Blooming in the Dark

Something Good to Remember: When your life overwhelms, His abundant grace overwhelms us all the more.

For Reflection: What out of the three suggestions (Receive, Focus, or Invite) can you work on this week if you find yourself drowning in the middle of pain?

> What do you need to receive from the Father?
>
> Are you spiraling and needing to refocus?
>
> Or do you need to invite people in so you're not fighting this battle alone?

For Meditation: Ephesians 3:14–21

To Pray: *Thank You, Lord, for Your abundance. Open my spiritual eyes to see Your love and blessings in my life even in the middle of unspeakable pain. Meet me here, in my broken state. I offer You whatever I have left and trust that You will be enough for me. "Let it be to me." Amen.*

chapter 2

When Insecurity Paralyzes You: Security in Christ

But you belong to God, my dear children. You have already won a victory over those people, because the Spirit who lives in you is greater than the spirit who lives in the world.

1 JOHN 4:4

Something Good Will Grow

As you learn to realize the depth of what belonging to Christ means, the place where you find your significance and security will shift.

Moving to our hobby farm, The Faithful Homestead, has been one of the most transformative events of my life. Besides the cute animals, hard work, and endless hours outside as a family, God has met me here in ways that I could have never dreamed.

I *found* myself here. It took giving up control, laying down every preconceived notion I had about myself, and having silence in the middle of nowhere. As I got away from the stresses and comfort of busy city life, I found myself alone with God in the space of our country property, and His great love for me began to settle in. In the process, I finally saw my value in Christ and who I am as a child of God. When God helped me see my significance, peace and clarity came upon me like a fresh spring rain, my joy was restored, and a heavy weight that I had never realized I was toiling under was miraculously lifted.

For the first time in my life, I felt deeply secure.

You'd think I would have already learned to place my value in Christ. I've been walking with the Lord for years. I even write Christian books! Unfortunately, insecurities have paralyzed me for far too long. I don't want that for you.

We're going to linger at His feet, look up, and get to the heart of our insecurities in this chapter.

Why do we lack confidence?

Why do we have such a difficult time grasping God's love for us?

Who does God say we are?

What good can actually grow from the insecurities that chase us?

Insecurity doesn't have to follow you all the way to glory. Let's address the lies Satan has whispered and truly walk in Christ's victory and truth. The more honest you are about your insecurities, the more you make space for God's truth to reshape your thinking. It's possible to stand on God's promises and character—regardless of your circumstances.

Recognizing Your Insecurities

Before moving to the farm, I equated mustered-up self-confidence with spiritual strength. I'd sweep my insecurities under the rug. Maybe you've done the same.

Insecurities can present themselves in many ways throughout our lives. Someone might say something that triggers a childhood wound. You might compare your life with someone else's on social media and find yourself feeling defeated and discontent. Maybe people have said some hurtful things to you or about you and you responded in an emotionally shaky way. Maybe you revert to people-pleasing so that the focus isn't on your flaws. Or maybe you're spiritually insecure and have heard that God has done big things for others, but don't believe God will do the same for you. Maybe you have a difficult past or physical attributes that you deem as negative.

Ultimately, each insecurity reveals where you've sought to find your worth: somewhere other than the person of Christ and the truth of His Word.

We can't fix ourselves, our wounds, or our insecurities without the help of the Holy Spirit. We can't mend what only God can heal. We can't see ourselves through the clear and holy lens of the Father if we are still trying to find our value through the shattered glass that is our life and painful, broken memories.

I understand what it's like to feel small because of insecurity. I am familiar with feeling less than. Sometimes these feelings were self-imposed. Other times, they were a response to the way others treated me, or my perception of their behavior. I responded to insecurity by internalizing the belief that speaking out against hurt or mistreatment was too dangerous. Letting insecurity silence me felt safer.

It has taken me years, and a lot of counseling, to regain my voice and see my value and worth in Christ.

The Bible doesn't give us much insight into the enemy's mind other than that it's his mission to steal, kill, and destroy the image-bearers of God (John 10:10), but it seems to me that he enjoys my insecurities. Keeping me feeling purposeless and worthless turns up the volume on lies and turns down the volume on the truth of who I am in Christ, keeping me in a cycle of insignificance, blind to my true identity in Christ. Can you identify with any of this?

You likely know the darkness that overcomes when your confidence is destroyed. Have you seen your self-esteem turn to ash right in front of you? When you lay your head down at night and tears stream down your face, it's not because the beauty you once had is gone or what was said about you hurt. It's because you were so deeply manipulated that you actually believe you are the dragon that blows the fire on the beauty of your own life. That's what the enemy wants us to believe. I've been there and I was convinced that I would never be enough.

Insecurity can be paralyzing and keep you from growing in Christ because you can't believe that you could ever bloom into a gorgeous flower. You think all that you are or will ever amount to is some pesky weed because you're viewing yourself through the wrong lens. Do you even comprehend the strength and beauty and value inside of you because of who Jesus is?

Your insecurities are keeping you from blooming into the unshakable disciple of Christ that you are called to be.

We have to allow the Lord to change our thoughts and beliefs about ourselves. Today. Invite the Holy Spirit to uproot the insecurities in your life by tracing the roots all the way back through the soil, and then completely cutting them off and tossing them out of your life. Your insecurities are keeping you from blooming into the unshakable disciple of Christ that you are called to be. We want to be so aligned with Him that our secure identity in Him is our firm foundation going forward.

What God Has Done for You

Where do we go from here? We start with knowing our kind and good Father. "Don't you see how wonderfully kind, tolerant, and patient God is with you? Does this mean nothing to you? Can't you see that his kindness is intended to turn you from your sin?" (Rom. 2:4).

What's really keeping you trapped in patterns of insecurity? Unbelief!

Do you really believe you are a child of God?

Do you believe you were made in His image?

Do you believe He has been kind to you?

Once you do, you will begin to walk in freedom. Not believing who you are as a child of God, made in His image, shows your unbelief. Not walking in the fullness of His freedom and victory is to reject His kindness. To not walk in the grace and value offered to us is diminishing His great sacrifice on the cross. We were bought at a high price. As we begin to understand this and let it take root, our insecurities will start to wither away.

If you are a follower of Jesus, the Father sees you through the lens of His Son.

He doesn't see the extra fifteen pounds that make you tug at your clothes.

He doesn't see the people around you and think they are smarter or more interesting.

He doesn't see your house as too small or your kitchen as outdated.

He doesn't see the parts of your personality you wish you could change.

He sees Jesus. Instead of constantly trying to fix the things that make you feel insecure, playing an exhausting game of whack-a-mole, ask for eyes to see yourself as God sees you.

Yes, God wants to change you, but not because He wants to highlight your insecurities to blame or shame you. His goal is to make you more like Jesus: perfection personified. This sanctification and refining often happens through trials and suffering. This in itself is interesting because it is those difficult seasons of trials and suffering that can bring on insecurity. Or we can choose to dwell on His work, not our shortcomings. He is refining. Growing. Teaching. Remaking.

I am so grateful that when God looks at me, He doesn't pick apart my outward appearance.

> The Lord doesn't see things the way you see them. People judge by outward appearance, but the Lord looks at the heart. (1 Sam. 16:7)

God goes directly to your heart and sees the real you. He's the only one who knows you, gets you, and understands every single part of your life and soul. He knows us so deeply because He divinely created us. And now when we look to Him, we find our true selves, the parts that matter for eternity. But we so easily forget our spiritual DNA because of the lies and opinions we cling to instead of listening to the One who has always been calling us closer and speaking truth over our lives.

We have to establish that we are already free from the power of rejection and shame because Christ already took it on the cross. "Yet it was our weaknesses he carried; it was our sorrows that weighed him down" (Isa. 53:4). If we don't understand what God has done for us, we're going to be spinning in circles with no place to land, always searching for someone or something to validate us. But there is only One who can turn the pain of one filled with insecurities to a purpose-filled woman who claims her King's victory as her own.

> We must be enveloped in the Word of God so that we know what our heavenly Father wants for us and who He says we are in Him.

From personal experience, this is not an instant, one-time win. It's a lifelong journey. The load becomes lighter when you accept that this is a process and surround yourself with a strong inner circle, those who have your back and who you do life with, who push you and encourage your heart toward truth. But it still takes time. That's why we must be enveloped in the Word of God so that we know what our heavenly Father thinks, what He wants for us, and who He says we are in Him. Knowing more about God's heart for you will be your first step into becoming unshakable and secure in Him.

God Is . . .

Whenever I find myself shaken or insecure, I go back to God's Word. Even if I'm trying to force myself to think positively, thinking too much about myself feeds self-absorption. My flesh is drawn to social media quizzes and posts that "type" me out and explain why I am the way that I am. Our flesh—that is, our sin nature—craves validation. But we don't need our insecurities to perpetuate more of our flesh and pride, and we sure can't be delivered from insecurity this way. Going to God's Word, meditating on His character, and remaining secure in His truth gets the focus off ourselves and on to our steadfast God.

God is:

Trustworthy (Ps. 20:7):
Because of this we can hold on to what He says about us.

Kind (Ps. 145:8–9):
Those negative and destructive thoughts in your head are not from the Lord.

Loving (John 3:16–17):
He gave His one and only Son to take your place. Grasping His perfect love is the ultimate confidence boost!

Faithful (2 Tim. 2:13):
Don't let insecurity convince you that God will abandon you. He won't.

Good (Ps. 107:1):
The enemy is the one who is out to steal, kill, and destroy everything good in your life, not God.

Defender (Ps. 18:1–2):
You don't have to prove yourself to anyone. You are to live for an audience of One. You can trust Him to defend you against the attacks and criticisms of others.

What a good and amazing God we serve! Knowing more about Him takes the pressure off us to be someone we're not. Knowing Him helps us see who we really are, as defined by our Creator and Savior.

I'm so thankful that I don't have to be my own defender or make my own peace. How about you? Second Thessalonians 1:6 says, "In his justice he will pay back those who persecute you." He has your back!

As His Child, I Am . . .

As Christians, we already know the truth of who God is. And the descriptors in the list above only scratch the surface! Maybe you can add more.

Then how about me? How about you? If we're in Christ, who are we? If the same powerful and sovereign God who conquered death also created you and me in His image and likeness, then we should never second-guess our identity in Him.

But we're human. From time to time, we all need reminders of who we are in Him. Moments of insecurity will come. For something good to grow, you will need to train your heart to see yourself through His eyes.

Find these verses in your Bible, read them in context, and pray that God would open your eyes to His love for you.

You are . . .

Made in His Image (Gen. 1:27):
His perfect, glorious, beautiful, matchless, divine image.

Chosen (1 Peter 2:9; Eph. 1:4, 11):
You were not an afterthought or an accident.

Set Apart (2 Tim. 1:9; Titus 3:5):
By grace you are called to live a set apart and holy life.

His Workmanship (Eph. 2:20):
You were expertly made.

New Creation (2 Cor. 5:17; Gal. 4:6–7):
You are no longer dead or gripped by shame and sin. You are alive with Christ, called and chosen.

Fearfully and Wonderfully Made (Ps. 139:14):
You were created with great care.

Precious and Loved (Col. 3:12; 1 Thess. 1:4):
You are worthy and valued.

Victorious (1 Cor. 15:57):
You are a conqueror, no longer defeated or unsuccessful.

Healed by His Wounds (1 Peter 2:24):
He already took your sin, shame, and sorrow. He will walk with you through every high and low.

Forgiven (Eph. 1:7):
You can now accept His free gift of salvation and walk in freedom.

Complete in Christ (Col. 2:10):
God is everything you need.

Adopted (Rom. 8:15; Eph. 1:5):
You are declared as HIS, a part of a family, given all of His blessings and promises, receiving full access to the Father and living under His authority.

Our Responsibility

You, my friend, are a delight—His delight.

With that understanding, we have to be careful and address the truth that knowing our worth does not give us permission to forgo any convictions the Holy Spirit impresses on us. We don't turn a blind eye to our responsibility of daily repentance. It's easy to swing from one extreme to the other, but the Lord wants us to live in a healthy balance of confidence and humility.

By no means does our value and worth in Christ overpower our need to still submit to Christ daily. There is a spiritually disciplined balance. Knowing our identity in Him does mean that the old self is dead and gone and the new self is at work in us by the power of the Holy Spirit. We have the privilege to live under a new authority, a new name, and a new way of life. Our security comes not from who we are (or were), but who He has transformed us to be.

When you truly understand who you are when you are adopted into the family of God, you can watch your insecurities bloom into His victory in your life.

When you committed your life to Christ, repented, confessed, and believed, your life was marked with victory. The banner over your life used to be one of shame and guilt. But now you are justified through the cross and are seen as enough because He is enough. The banner over your life is grace and love!

When we truly understand who we are when we are adopted into the family of God, our faulty confidence we once had blooms into an unshakable confidence, deeply rooted in truth. You can watch your insecurities bloom into His victory in your life. What a sacred and undeserved exchange.

> Can anything ever separate us from Christ's love? Does it mean he no longer loves us if we have trouble or calamity, or are persecuted, or hungry, or destitute, or in danger, or threatened with death? . . . No, despite all these things, overwhelming victory is ours through Christ, who loved us. (Rom. 8:35, 37)

No words, no painful circumstances, no hardship, and no one can separate you from Christ's love. You are chosen, on purpose, with intrinsic value, to glorify Him all the days of your life.

Practically Healing from Hurt

Over my years in ministry, I have come in contact with many women who are fighting silent battles in their mind because of the lies they tell themselves or the lies they are told by others. I understand this hurt. When someone tries to tear me down with their words or actions, I am still learning to put my confidence in the knowledge that the Lord watches over the path of the godly (Ps. 1:6) and that He defines and cares for me.

So much of our insecurities stem from shame. However, we have to remind ourselves that when Jesus died and rose again, the devil's power was broken (Col. 2:14–15). Satan doesn't have the power to intimidate you and to shame you into believing you are not worthy or enough. Because of Christ, and in Him, you are worthy! Next time someone takes credit for your work or lies about you behind your back, you don't need to jump in and defend yourself. With confidence in Christ, we can learn to let go of what no longer defines or concerns us. God sees. The more we practice what we preach and live out who we are in Him, the easier it becomes to stay grounded and confident in who we are. He replaces our insecurities with security in Him.

We know the truth of who God is and who we are in Him. We know our talents and quirks and blemishes and giftings, and it's time to embrace who God has created us to be! Called, loved, adopted. His. Not hiding in shame any longer. When we embrace our uniqueness in Christ, we don't crave validation from others. Sometimes living in His victory is as simple as recognizing your shortcomings, repenting of the lies you have believed, replacing them with truth, and moving on.

We cannot isolate when we are struggling but must confront our insecurities head-on. Surround yourself with people who call you to be better.

A way to live this out is to be honest with a friend or spouse with how you're *really* doing. Insecurities can get in the way of your involvement in the church or community and your growth. That's why it's important to get into a Bible study, prayer group, mom get-together, or even a weekly check-in with a good friend. We cannot isolate when we are struggling but must confront our insecurities head-on. Surrounding yourself with people who call you to be better (e.g., forgiving, walking in victory, daily accountability) and establishing boundaries for those who perpetuate cycles of insecurities in our lives will change you for the better.

One of the roots of my insecurity was distortion of the Word through spiritual manipulation. I was told that Christian phrases like "turn the other cheek" or "be at peace with everyone" applied to all situations. It wasn't until I really dug into the Word myself and received godly wisdom from counselors that I understood that God was not telling me to endure abuse or accept other people's sin for the sake of peace.

Maybe you've been told similar things. Maybe your definition of *peace* needs to be rooted in boundaries or saying no or calling others to accountability. For example, in Matthew 5:39 ("If someone slaps you on the right cheek, offer the other cheek also"), Jesus is telling us to live without always being offended and taking the persecution of others without seeking vengeance in anger. He's not literally saying to let people repeatedly slap us!

Yes, love is patient and kind and keeps no record of wrongs, but love also does not rejoice in injustice but instead it rejoices whenever the *truth* wins out (1 Cor. 13:4–6). Definitions and meaning matter. Don't let other people confuse truth in order to keep you paralyzed in shame and insecurities. What the enemy has done since the beginning of time is twist Scripture to deceive and to shame. Deception is the enemy's nature. Don't buy it. Let's be women of the Word, who truly know our Bibles so that we can walk securely in Him.

When we know the truth of who God is and who we are in Him, we're able to reject distortions of truth from the enemy that were meant to silence and shame us and instead stand on the truth of what verses and phrases like those above actually mean. Living in His victory is available to you!

Speak the Truth Out Loud

One of my favorite practices as of late is reading Ephesians 1 every morning. Before I start my day, I say these truths from Ephesians 1 out loud. You can join me in doing this!

> He blesses me with every spiritual gift. (v. 3)
>
> He loved me before the world was made. (v. 4)
>
> He chose me in Christ to be holy. (v. 4)
>
> He decided in advance to adopt me—He wanted to do this and it gave Him great pleasure! (v. 5)
>
> He pours out His glorious grace on me. (v. 6)
>
> He purchased my freedom. (v. 7)
>
> He forgave me. (v. 7)
>
> He showers His kindness on me. (v. 8)
>
> He showers me with all wisdom and understanding. (v. 8)
>
> He reveals His plan through Christ for me. (v. 9)
>
> I am united with Christ and received an inheritance. (v. 11)
>
> He chose me in advance and makes everything work out in my life according to His plan. (v. 11)

He identifies me as His own. (v. 13)

He gave me the Holy Spirit—His guarantee that He will give us the inheritance He promised. (v. 14)

He purchased me so I could glorify Him. (v. 14)

Thank You, Jesus!

How do we get past insecurities? By not proving or striving or forcing or pretending. Jesus defines us. We trust who He says we are, which enables us to reject the lies spoken to us or about us. We remain so tethered to our Creator that every word passes through Him first before we receive anything into our hearts and minds. We pray for wisdom and discernment to take responsibility and accountability for our missteps and recognize that we need Jesus, moment by moment each and every day. We live humbly, knowing that our only security comes from our gracious Lord.

Now, extend grace to yourself. When you apologize for things you never did so that you can keep the peace. When you're made to feel like you are never enough: never good enough, never spiritual enough, never smart enough, never pretty enough. When someone breaks you down so that they can feel better about themselves. When you believe the enemy's lies over the Lord's truths. When you feel guilted into diminishing yourself to make everyone else happy . . . Remember who you are in Christ.

He sees all. Remember who He says you are and what He has clothed you in. Remember Ephesians 1. Remember you are valued, precious, loved, His workmanship, and a new creation. Remember He has your back. You do matter. You are whole in Christ, and you are already victorious because of what Christ has already done. Insecurities can flee; it is finished.

Blooming in the Dark

Something Good to Remember: Your security comes from who Jesus says you are.

For Reflection: When you read the list of who God is, do you doubt any? What trait about yourself do you not fully believe?

For Meditation: Ephesians 1:3–14

To Pray: *Lord, thank You that You are my victory and secure place of peace! Thank You for taking all my sin, shame, and sorrows on the cross when I deserved it all. Thank You for creating me in Your image and for calling me by name. Now I humbly ask that I see myself how You see me, Lord. Break the chains of insecurity and guard me in Your victory and strength. Amen.*

chapter 3

When You're Lonely and Left Out: Comfort in Christ

For the more we suffer for Christ, the more God will shower us with his comfort through Christ.

2 CORINTHIANS 1:5

Something Good Will Grow

As you learn to be comforted in Christ alone, you will grow in strength and servanthood

Over the course of my life, I have been "the new girl" more often than not. My family moved a lot for my father's job while I was growing up, so I frequently found myself in a new neighborhood, a new school, and a new church with new friends, new classmates, and new teammates. My experiences in my college years mirrored my childhood as I transferred universities, changed majors, and moved states.

Being the new girl when I was young meant that I walked into countless classrooms with children who had grown up together and already had family friends cemented in their lives. These kids already had community and deep friendships while I was just the tall girl from another state.

I joined sports teams where all I had in common with the players was our mutual love for the sport. The other players often had years of experience playing together. Due to their already deeply forged bonds, nothing I could do would get me an invitation into their inner circle.

Always new and feeling out of place, I felt lonely despite being surrounded by people. I know you've felt the same.

Later, as a young married mother with a husband in medicine, I found myself in a similar position with lots of relocation. Medical school, residency, fellowship and/or the first job post-training are often all in different states and locations. Each time we moved, I was forced again to face many new somethings. New town. New church. New school. New friends. New everything. In fact, every single one of our four children was born in a different hospital, in a different city, and came home to a different house.

Always new.

Walk Forward and Bless

We've all experienced loneliness, being left out, or feeling less than. Maybe you even experienced it at some point this week.

The birthday dinner you had expected to be invited to.

The old friend you grew up with who suddenly avoids you.

The new friend who never texted you back.

The mom group that made plans without you.

It hurts to be left out and it's almost impossible to "just get over it" or forget how painful it is. We can't will our way to feeling better, because it's so much deeper than merely not being invited to something. Someone you were beginning to trust and value forgot you. Being accidentally forgotten is painful. Being intentionally forgotten is even worse. Not only were you caught off guard when you were left out, but now you're forced to recognize that the value you placed on the relationship was not reciprocated. That's when the loneliness settles in.

One of our deepest desires in relationships is to be known. We all adore our longtime friends and family who "get us." They know what we're thinking and why we do what we do. They know what to get us for our birthday and how we respond when stressed. These people are rare. But when other people are not seeing us for who we are or making an intentional effort to show they care, we can find ourselves going to dark places. We start blaming ourselves, thinking something is wrong with us, becoming bitter or unforgiving, losing hope for future friendships, or all of the above.

How do we stop ourselves from taking things personally and having a fear of loneliness? Walk forward and bless.

When this happens, we start placing our value in how people include us and see us instead of finding value in our Creator, our only true Comforter. This is why discussing our insecurities and walking in victory in the previous chapter was so important.

How do we get out of this cycle? How do we stop ourselves from taking things personally and having a fear of loneliness? Where is our place when there are cliquey friend groups, people who don't get you, you're feeling isolated without community, family moves, or job changes? Walk forward and bless. We walk forward in our sorrow while blessing others right where we are.

I know that sounds easier said than done, and it is. It is both simple and difficult. However, it is imperative that we learn to practically live this out while allowing God to be our comfort in loneliness.

It Starts with Jesus

I can't imagine how Jesus felt during His time on earth. On one hand, He was fully God, all-knowing, sovereign, perfect and sinless in every way and in all He did. On the other hand, He was fully man, preaching all over Israel, making friends, having lots of followers, and was a pretty popular guy. And yet He was misunderstood. There was no one, not a friend, not a follower, not His mother, not a disciple, who could truly understand what He was walking and the burden He had to bear.

The emotions of knowing about His future crucifixion would be unbearable for any one of us. He was carrying the weight and burdens of the world, wanting so desperately for all of humanity to know Him and place their trust in Him, but also loving people enough to let them choose and have free will. He watched betrayal through Judas and saw Peter deny Him. He was second-guessed, and others didn't follow through when He needed rest. People doubted Him or didn't appreciate Him, and countless times His words went right over their heads.

It must have felt lonely at times, living set apart, and being like no other who had ever lived.

Yet, He was always comforted by the Father. Jesus went to Him, went off alone to seek Him out, and was refueled and ultimately comforted by His time in His Father's presence.

In Matthew 26, Jesus went to the garden of Gethsemane to pray just before He was arrested. He was distressed and even told the disciples who were with Him, "My soul is crushed with grief to the point of death." What strong words! Jesus was in anguish over the coming crucifixion. "He went on a little farther and bowed his face to the ground, praying, 'My Father! If it is possible, let this cup of suffering be taken away from me. Yet I want your will to be done, not mine'" (vv. 36–39).

This shows us that even in an intense moment of His affliction, having a soul filled with sorrow, Jesus still bowed down, prayed, lamented, petitioned, and then ended with, "Yet I want your will to be done, not mine." He found comfort, strength, and peace by going to the Father because He knew true comfort could only be found in His Father's presence and believing God's sovereign plan to save humanity.

Do we follow in Jesus' footsteps by submitting and going to the Father in the same way? Where do we go for comfort? I think it's safe to say that we often don't run to our heavenly Father first when we feel lonely or left out. We might turn to whoever will listen, find a documentary or movie or series to binge, or overindulge in food or unhealthy amounts of online shopping.

What or who you turn to in your loneliness matters immensely. These worldly choices can often sound harmless. But it's in these small moments of seemingly insignificant decisions that you have the power by the Holy Spirit to say yes to the Father and turn to Him. If you choose satisfaction and contentment in Him, your choice will define you and grow you in ways you never thought possible.

These small shifts in our day will become the spiritual habits that carry us through the rest of our lives.

It's the small choices. The next right step. God uses these wise and daily disciplines to shape us. Remind yourself of who you are in Christ. Go back to the list from chapter 2 and "speak the truth out loud." It's a discipline that takes some practice, but learning to posture our hearts toward Him in our loneliness will bring us the satisfying comfort in Christ we've been searching for. How do we do this? By believing and trusting God's sovereign plan over our lives as Jesus did in the garden of Gethsemane.

These small shifts in our day will become the spiritual habits that carry us through the rest of our lives. Then one day when you face a bout of loneliness, while the old you would have felt left out and turned to something unsatisfactory for comfort, the new you knows who she is in Christ, recites a Bible verse from memory that helps her turn to God, and then invites a new neighbor over for coffee.

Turning to Christ *first* and trusting His plan when you're left out and lonely will bring you the lasting comfort you craved from the beginning. Turning to God for your comfort is going to change your life. But it doesn't stop there. He's then going to use you in your loneliness to be an outpouring and comfort to others.

It Continues with Jesus

Let's read 2 Corinthians 1:3–7 (ESV) and break down the comfort we receive when sufferings come.

> Blessed be the God and Father of our Lord Jesus Christ, the Father of mercies and God of all comfort, who comforts us in all our affliction, so that we may be able to comfort those who are in any affliction, with the comfort with which we ourselves are comforted by God. For as we share abundantly in Christ's sufferings, so through Christ we share abundantly in comfort too. If we are afflicted, it is for your comfort and salvation; and if we are comforted, it is for your comfort, which you experience when you patiently endure the same sufferings that we suffer. Our hope for you is unshaken, for we know that as you share in our sufferings, you will also share in our comfort.

I know these verses are a little repetitive, but that was intentional by the author so that we can understand the importance of being comforted by God. We can spot three major takeaways that stand out in that passage.

The first is that *God comforts us in our loneliness and sufferings so that we may be able to comfort others.* We serve a generous God, but when He lavishes His grace and comfort and love on us, He finds great joy when we in turn give that to others.

The second is that *we share abundantly in both suffering and comfort through Christ.* Walking in sorrow continues to show me the beautiful exchange of giving the Lord my heartache and watching Him pour out His abundance of comfort. Even in the hard places of loneliness, His comfort overwhelms us all the more.

Then, *we patiently endure the trials of loneliness.* Endure is a verb, and a synonym is *brave* as a verb. As we pray for doors to open, people to love and serve, new friends and opportunities, to be comforted and not forgotten, we patiently *brave* these trials.

David Guzik's commentary on 2 Corinthians 1 says, "The idea behind this word for *comfort* in the New Testament is always more than soothing sympathy. It has the idea of strengthening, of helping, of making strong. The idea behind this word is communicated by the Latin word for comfort (*fortis*), which also means 'brave.'"[1] We become courageous in our loneliness to seek opportunity and not just wait around for life to happen to us.

We are comforted by the only One who can make us strong, who can help us and who will strengthen us in the midst of our loneliness. Brave the loneliness, endure, and allow God to give you the courage to be the initiator. Step out in your sorrow. Make it your mission to befriend someone else. We're not stepping out because we're coming from a place of fear of loneliness, but because we have experienced Christ as our comfort and we want in turn to comfort others.

I love how the New Living Translation puts 2 Corinthians 1:5: "For the more we suffer for Christ, the more God will shower us with his comfort through Christ." The unique suffering that stems from loneliness is something we'll all walk through at some time, but this verse is something we can stand on, trusting that God will shower us with His comfort through Christ because of what we are walking through.

With Christ, comfort is coming *because* of the loneliness.

Rise Above the Hurt

I rarely forget a face. If I've had a conversation with you longer than just a quick introduction, the next time I see you, I will make it a point to say hello and might even give you a hug. But if I meet someone and then a week later that very same person comes up to me and says, "Hi, have I met you before?" a part of me feels hurt.

This has happened to me multiple times. What I've come to understand is that not everyone has the same giftings, and that's okay. Not everyone is visual and can remember a face. Not everyone remembers names or something specific about you after meeting for the first time. (I'm great with faces but bad at names.) Deep down, we just want to be known, remembered, and valued. But something we can all work on is not taking perceived slights so personally.

> *Working through loneliness is less about taking things personally and more about being open to other opportunities.*

At the end of the day, you have to remain confident in who you are in Christ so that you don't get sidetracked by petty things, regardless of why or how you were left out. There are dozens of people who would be beyond blessed to have you in their life!

We can't let other people's shortcomings affect our days. When I think about being unshakable amidst the pain of loneliness, it's less about taking things personally and more about being open to other opportunities. Maybe you weren't invited to a gathering you would have enjoyed. Rather than dwell on your disappointment, find someone else who'd like to be included in a get-together. Invite her over for coffee. You'll both have a great time! You're not invalidating your hurt but being stronger than letting it defeat you, and allowing God to use these times of loneliness for our good and His glory!

Loneliness Brought Contentment

I remember when we first moved to our small country town with a population of—get ready for it—six hundred people. I about lost it. For starters, I'm just going to be honest, the front of our house is not cute. It's not magazine worthy by any means and I can't tell you how many stink bugs I've killed, the number of times I've stepped in chicken poop on our walkway, or how many cobwebs I've swept. When I went to my first ever "sale barn" to see the livestock for sale that week, I had never felt so out of place in my entire life. It was an experience.

For the first several months, I felt extremely lonely. Every single person we met was so kind and would give you the shirt off their back, but we didn't know anything about farm living and were like the proverbial petunia in an onion patch, just some city folks in the country. Plus, everyone we met already had their own deeply woven pasts like my experience with childhood classmates, and I felt it. Everyone's parents had grown up together, all went to the same family church, kids went to the same schools, and some even lived on the same property as the generations before them. The roots are deep in the country and I felt like an outsider who didn't belong.

Have you ever heard the phrase "the grass is greenest where you water it"? That's exactly how it is with loneliness. You can convince yourself the grass is greener elsewhere, complaining, "My life would have been so much better if I was just invited, or just lived in this neighborhood, or just had a close friend, or just lived in a bigger city." But until we understand we are planted where we are for a *reason*, we'll never have the opportunity to allow Christ to work through us in our loneliness.

Until we understand we are planted where we are for a reason, we'll never have the opportunity to allow Christ to work through us in our loneliness.

Loneliness is where I learned contentment. That might sound odd at first but sometimes you need to get away from the cycle of being busy, people-pleasing, and juggling friendships in order to get quiet before the Lord and come to the realization that He is all you truly have and need. I didn't feel close with anyone during the first six months after we moved out in the country except for my husband, children, and animals. But in that loneliness, there was space to think and to quiet my mind. I was given the time to reevaluate what I want and to prayerfully consider each relationship. I was able to sit back and watch God work because I couldn't force anything. And in those first six months when I basically wanted to look up new houses and new jobs because I felt so out of place where I was, I humbled myself and trusted that God knew what He was doing. *Yet I want Your will to be done, not mine*, I was learning to say.

Part of allowing God to comfort us is by trusting Him first. Just like Jesus in the garden of Gethsemane. Above all else, He trusted that His Father's plan far exceeded His present torment. We have to believe the same in our personal stories.

Life Together

A few months after we moved in, we held a Friday Farm Night. As I mentioned, we didn't know anyone, so I thought it would be fun to invite anyone and everyone over for a backyard dinner. I ordered barbecue, borrowed the church's folding tables and chairs, strung some lights, filled tiny antique glass vases with flowers, and invited a bunch of people over. I even invited the woman from the barbecue joint who took my order over the phone because, why not? The more the merrier. I desperately wanted to meet people.

Life is better with people. Of course, it's messier and more chaotic at times!

And you know what happened? We had over fifty people come with their families. Kids were running barefoot all over the place, catching lightning bugs and playing hide-and-go-seek. The kids stayed up way past their bedtime and God ended the evening by giving us the most beautiful sunset I've ever seen.

Moral of the story: You belong in community and not alone. Life is better with people. Of course, it's messier and more chaotic at times, but we need the body of believers to walk with us. I understand that there are seasons where God wants you to be more alone to teach you and heal you and build you back up. But then when it's time, we need to become the initiator. Be confident enough to engage and invite people, even when you're the new one. Though you may feel lonely, challenge yourself to be the first one to reach out.

That night was so much fun. Out of that evening came wonderful friendships and connections, laughter and fellowship. We simply had to stop waiting around to be invited to something as the new people in town and take a step forward ourselves. Yes, there might be rejection. Yes, people may bail. But we have to believe whoever is supposed to show up will be there. I'd encourage you to try. I promise you that there are people out there who would love to be invited to something. Isn't that God's design for us? Living life with people, being an offering to the Lord, and getting outside of our bubbles to proclaim His faithfulness?

I know you have been burned by people who forgot about you. I know it feels like no one understands you. I know it's lonely when you went from three really close friends nearby to no one but your immediate family—or even just yourself. I know what that feels like but it's time to trust in the Lord's plan for you, recognizing that even in this place of loneliness He still has something for you to learn and areas of your character and faith to grow. God will use even our loneliness for His glory.

I will always look back on that first Farm Night with such fondness because I had no idea who would show up. I had no idea if we'd have enough food—or too much if no one came—or if the weather would cooperate. But God did so much out of our small offering. Once again, I gave Him whatever I could in my loneliness, and He lavished His comfort on me through that evening. What a special reminder I'll have the rest of my life.

I can honestly say I am thankful to have been the new one who felt out of place, lonely and left out at times growing up. It took me awhile to get here, but it was through the pain of loneliness that I learned the incomprehensible comfort of Christ. Then out of the comfort I received, I learned my role in finding deep connection with others. We were not meant to live life alone.

Blooming in the Dark

Something Good to Remember: We walk forward in our loneliness, and pray that God would use us to include someone else who's lonely and feeling left out.

For Reflection: Who is someone you can invite over this week? Maybe a playdate with other moms and their kids. Maybe a double date with your spouse. Maybe a family who just had a new baby. Maybe an empty nester whose home was once filled with activity. Maybe just a new friend who pops in for a cup of coffee. It doesn't have to be extravagant. Let's be brave!

For Meditation: 2 Corinthians 1:3–7

To Pray: *Lord, thank You that You are the God of all comfort. Thank You that when I feel insignificant, lonely, and left out, You are there to comfort me and remind me where my hope and value are found. I pray that You would bring opportunities for me to bless and include others, even in my loneliness. Amen.*

chapter 4

When Fathers Fail: Tenderness in Christ

The LORD is like a father to his children,
tender and compassionate to those who fear him.

PSALM 103:13

Something Good Will Grow

As you learn to see God as a loving and attentive Father, trust in His care and freedom from painful independence will grow in you.

No one has a perfect dad. People will fail us because we're all human and life is filled with evil and sin. You've failed someone and I've failed someone, but a father-daughter relationship is a unique and important connection. We pray to a "heavenly Father," not a "heavenly mother." One of the ways your view of your earthly father affects you most deeply is because it impacts your view of God.

Your father may have wanted a son. Your father may have traveled a lot. Your father may have been overcome with addiction or alcoholism. Your father may have walked out on your family. Maybe you never knew your real dad and lacked a connection to a father. Even if he was by the world's standard a "good dad," he still had shortcomings. Maybe he was kind, but not generous. Maybe supportive, but not a good leader.

In response, we daughters often overcompensate. We try to prove ourselves but fall into the same addictions. We don't trust men and we have low self-esteem. Some of us people-please excessively, crave love, or attempt to find value in anyone or anything. This is not healthy and proves how vital it is to not get our views of our earthly father and heavenly Father twisted.

God's plan is that husbands and fathers are the ones who lead our families and our churches. When this standard is disrupted by bad examples, you can see how damaging it can be to a flourishing life as God's daughter. I have personally seen how the distorted beliefs I had in certain seasons of life kept me from believing the truth of God's tender, loving character.

I don't want that for you. Something had to change for me, and something has to change for you.

God Is Better

When people who should care tenderly for us fail, and it causes us to run from a tender relationship with Christ, we have a problem. Let me start by reminding you of something: God is better than any fatherly example you have or have had in your life. He is infinitely better.

For many years I didn't believe that truth, so I didn't run to my heavenly Father when walking through hardships. This isn't abnormal if you didn't have a good example of what a father's love looks like. You can easily put false learned behaviors onto God if you've experienced too much shame, anger, or misunderstanding. That leads to avoiding drawing close to God because of your lack of trust. When you have a negative idea of who God is, it's scary to run to Him with all your pain, questions, needs, or even gratitude.

Maybe you've felt rejected. Maybe when you asked questions, you didn't receive honest answers in return. Maybe when you craved love and support, you got the cold shoulder. Maybe you've never seen a kind, patient, and faithful example of a loving father so you view God through a harsh and angry lens. When your examples haven't been Christlike, then you hesitate to freely go to your heavenly Father, as you may believe He will exhibit the same qualities as a disappointing father in the flesh.

It's no wonder we think God will reject His daughters if we're honest with Him about how we're really feeling. It's no wonder why we think if we ask questions, we'll get chastised or pushed aside. When we desire God's love, it's no wonder we feel like we have to earn it or prove ourselves first before receiving what we desperately need.

Our perception of God is off. And when we then misrepresent God to others out of a false understanding of His character, we're not being faithful stewards of the grace He has bestowed upon us. If we don't know who God really is, we will not be able to talk about God in a healthy way with our kids, friends, and those He has entrusted to us.

We must understand the gentleness and love of our heavenly Father and protect that at all costs so that a distortion of God's character doesn't seep into our identity, community, church, and relationships.

Our heavenly Father sent His only Son—when we least deserved it—to take our sin and hurt and shame and guilt and everything we did and will ever do to the cross so that we can experience life abundantly with a glorious eternity ahead, free of all sin, hurt, shame, and pain.

Here's how the Bible says it:

> And we have seen and we testify that the Father has sent his Son to be the Savior of the world. (1 John 4:14 ESV)

That is love. That is a Father's deep love, and His love doesn't stop at the cross. James 1:17 (ESV) declares:

> Every good and perfect gift is from above, coming down from the Father of lights, with whom there is no variation or shadow due to change.

The Father pours out His grace, goodness, and love on you every day as He molds you into something beautiful that reflects His glory. What an abundant love!

Fully Loved. Fully Adopted.

I had an idea of God, and it was wrong.

Anger over grace
Blame over support
Shame over love
Harsh words over gentleness
Selfishness over servanthood
Condemnation over truth

But that isn't God as the Bible reveals Him. His Word shows us that we can completely flip the script:

> God is generous in grace (Eph. 1:7–9) and slow to anger (Ex. 34:6).
>
> The Lord longs to show you compassion, not blame you (Matt. 9:36).
>
> He wants to replace your shame with the joy of knowing you are deeply loved (Isa. 61:7).
>
> God is selfless and showed His great love for us by sending Christ to die for us (Rom. 5:8), and He showers us with kindness (Eph. 1:8).

> God doesn't reject us because we are broken, but before He made the world, He loved us and chose us in Christ to be holy and without fault in His eyes (Eph. 1:4).

I know it's painful to pull apart the false knowledge you once thought was correct about God and choose to trust Him to piece everything back together. But God is not severe or harsh. He is gentle and loving. Yes, He is a God of judgment, who must punish sin and call His children to holiness. But He is also a God of compassion, love, and grace, constantly calling His daughters back to Himself.

You are not made to live small. You are not made for mere scraps from heaven or to plead for love.

> He quiets you when your life is full of angst and chaos. (Zeph. 3:17)
>
> He walks with you when you're alone and don't know where to go. (Deut. 31:6)
>
> He has good things for you and wants to lavish His blessings on your life. (Rom. 8:28)
>
> He is guiding you and strengthening you with Himself when you feel weak. (Isa. 41:10)
>
> He provides, protects, and is full of wisdom and holiness. (Phil. 4:19)
>
> He's waiting with open arms whenever you want to run back to Him. (Luke 15:11–32)

There is no father like our Father.

Your life is about bringing glory to your heavenly Father, but that does not mean you get the leftovers. You are not meant to go sit in a corner and beg for someone to notice you. You are not made to live small. You are not made for mere scraps from heaven or to plead for love. You gave your life to Christ and you are now adopted into the family of God. Paul wrote about this in his letter to the Galatians.

> But when the set time had fully come, God sent his Son, born of a woman, born under the law, to redeem those under the law, that we might receive adoption to sonship. Because you are his sons, God sent the Spirit of his Son into our hearts, the Spirit who calls out, *"Abba*, Father." So you are no longer a slave, but God's child; and since you are his child, God has made you also an heir. (Gal. 4:4–7 NIV)

Did you notice who sent Jesus? The Father! He wants you to be adopted into His family. Do you know what that means? God has called you His own, His child. His daughter. Chosen, anointed, and holy, reaping all the authority and benefits of His heavenly kingdom. You are set apart for a specific purpose and have value.

So many of us are still living like we are unloved kids, not fully adopted. We act as though we are trees without roots, never fully embraced or accepted into a family, living with no foundation or security or plan. We rely on our own strength because too many people have failed us. We have no one to share our burdens, no one to turn to when life is hard, no one to rejoice with us or weep with us. We live as if our lives are meaningless, and no one cares.

You don't have to live like this any longer. God doesn't want you to just "get through" life. He wants to be the biggest part of your life, because in Him you have the fullness of His glory and life abundant! When you are His, adopted into the family of God, you carry all benefits. What's His is yours. The glorious eternity and inheritance are yours. God sees you through the lens of His perfect Son and wants you to share in His good things.

You belong.

What we believe about God defines us. How we view ourselves

in the family of God will either create lifelong insecurities or a secure identity rooted in the finished work of Jesus on the cross. If you've committed your life to Christ, you are adopted, loved, and you are His.

Discipline Is Love

If a father never disciplines his child and allows them to do whatever they want to do, eat whatever they want to eat, and speak however they want to speak, then that child grows to be an unruly, unhealthy, and selfish human. It also shows the lack of care and value the father has for that child by creating an environment with no discipline. A lack of fatherly discipline is not a blessing in any way; it shows a lack of love and effort. You become "not worth the hassle" in the eyes of a parent who has no desire to discipline.

> True contentment is found in full dependence on a faithful and good God who wants to make us more like His Son.

With God as our heavenly Father, we can be thankful He cares enough about our holiness to help us endure hardships with grace and wrapped in His strength. Discipline doesn't have to be a negative, but rather something that proves His love and care for us. Because He delights in us, God sees discipline as the necessary next step for your growth and sanctification. The goal is to be made more like Christ. If we can't take constructive discipline, then out of our own selfishness and pride we choose to go our own way, rejecting the pure love of our heavenly Father who wants what is good in our lives.

Enduring hardships and having discipline is proof that you are His child. He corrects those He cares for. God wants you moving toward holiness. If you are spiritually feeling the sin squeezed out of you, and the uncomfortable sifting that comes from His discipline, then know you are loved.

While we cannot confuse God's discipline as being the same as the evil and pain that enters our life from being residents of a fallen and broken world, sometimes we do bring hardships upon ourselves. But still, God is so good that He uses even those times as lessons and a way to draw you closer to Him. In other words: "'My child, don't make light of the LORD's discipline, and don't give up when he corrects you. For the LORD disciplines those he loves, and he punishes each one he accepts as his child.' As you endure this divine discipline, remember that God is treating you as his own children" (Heb. 12:5–7).

I know this is opposite of what the world teaches. The world completely distorts the idea that a loving Father disciplines those who are His, those He loves and cares for. Without understanding the loving act of discipline, our society chooses to celebrate a child's freedom to be whoever they want and act however they want. The repercussions are then confusing to an insecure child being pushed into the wind by selfish parents who find validation in their own pride and freedom. Both end up flailing, seeking validation and fulfillment in their own independence. Yet, we know true contentment is found in full dependence on a faithful and good God who wants to make us more like His Son.

Remember, our hardships are holy, meaning each painful thing that comes our way is an opportunity to become more like Christ and share in His sufferings. It doesn't mean our hardships are enjoyable or prayed for. No, you're crazy if you pray for pain! But it does mean God is over all. And when we rest in this sovereign Fatherly attribute of God, we know He has good things for us, even in the hardships.

God loves you. While it *feels* like God is sitting high and uninvolved, dropping devastation on you to make you holy, know that He understands you and is close. By sending His Son, God set the example that death breeds resurrection and life. Out of His kindness and love, God wants to walk with you through whatever you are facing.

We are not only growing through our trials, but we are being gently guided to the Father's heart in our pain. He is a tender, loving Father, and I see this more and more as trials continue to come through my life.

But I had this wrong for too long. I looked at God from the perspective of, "If I do x, y, and z, then He'll love me." Doesn't the Bible say to draw near to God and He'll draw near to you? Obey Him, and He'll bless you? Obey His commands, die to self, leave everything for His sake, then He'll love you and bless you and draw near to you and show His love? It felt like my relationship with God started with me.

My first step . . .

My obedience . . .

My drawing near . . .

My giving up . . .

I was overwhelmed with my own expectations and pressures to be perfect and have everything right.

As I was dealing with so much pain in life from people and circumstances, I couldn't carry it all. As I tried to be independent and strived to do everything on my own, I felt as if the cost to follow Christ outweighed the closeness and tender affection I ever felt from Him. I felt like I was carrying the weight of the relationship with God, as if everything good that came into my life was His response to my obedience. When I looked at my relationship with God in that way, I became like a soldier following orders, not a beloved daughter of the Most High King.

I thought God was only pleased in my doing, and if I wasn't accomplishing all my roles and responsibilities perfectly, He would be disappointed. That is so far from the truth. God isn't delighted in our "doing" and all the good works we strive to do.

While a wonderful outflow of our changed heart is to want to serve and glorify Him, God is simply delighted in us because He created us. "The Lord's delight is in those who fear him, those who put their hope in his unfailing love" (Ps. 147:11).

The purpose of our life is to become more like Christ but the pain of my misunderstanding of God's love outweighed the daily love or grace I desperately craved. Notice I'm saying "I feel" or "I felt" a lot. Feelings have a place, but they should not be the driving force behind what we think or do. Truth wins. His grace wins. God's character and love for you wins.

I'll say it again: your father and heavenly Father are different. When we marry the two beliefs together to construct an idea of who God is to us, we likely misunderstand His heart.

Our Good Shepherd

We recently rescued a mama sheep and her two little two-week-old lambs that were living in rough conditions and brought them home to our farm. As we cared for them, cleaned them up, and nursed them back to life, I was reminded of Psalm 23.

> The LORD is my shepherd;
>   I have all that I need.
> He lets me rest in green meadows;
>   he leads me beside peaceful streams.
>   He renews my strength;
> He guides me along right paths,
>   bringing honor to his name.
> Even when I walk
>   through the darkest valley
> I will not be afraid,
>   for you are close beside me.
> Your rod and your staff
>   protect and comfort me.
> You prepare a feast for me
>   in the presence of my enemies.
> You honor me by anointing my head with oil.
>   My cup overflows with blessings.

> Surely your goodness and unfailing love will pursue me
> all the days of my life,
> and I will live in the house of the Lord
> forever.

That is our loving Father—our good, kind, and tender loving Father. I know you might be in the middle of piecing back together who God is right now, or rediscovering how great He has always been, but I promise you He will guide you. God is with you and for you, loving you every step of the way. He provides all that you need. He brings you rest and gently guides and protects you. He renews your strength and is your peace. God's goodness and mercy will follow you all the days of your life.

Our Good Shepherd, our heavenly Father, knows what we need and when we need it.

Out of all of our farm animals, we were told that sheep are the most fragile and the weakest. We definitely see that to be true. They have to be handled differently, easily become stressed, and are the most vulnerable to outside predators. Yet, our Good Shepherd, our heavenly Father, knows this about us, His sheep, and He gently guides us with His tender, loving care. He knows what we need and when we need it. He knows how we're wired, what we're going to walk through, and He knows everything about us. Honestly, it brings me to tears as I write this: I have such a good Father! I hope and pray you see your heavenly Father this way as well. I don't always have a perfect view of Him and I still have moments where I place false characterizations on God. But by knowing and believing His Word, a fresh trust in His character is starting to grow.

He will feed His flock like a shepherd. He will carry the lambs in His arms, holding them close to His heart. He will gently lead the mother sheep with her young (Isa. 40:11).

I know you can't just wake up one day and have a perfect view of God. I know you can't erase all the father wounds or experiences that have accumulated over time and simply move on. I know it'll take a conscious effort and repentance if you struggle with pride and independence. But I promise you this: The more you invest and surrender in your relationship with God, the more secure and close and trusting you will be in Christ. He is a tender and loving and faithful Father.

One step at a time.

Blooming in the Dark

Something Good to Remember: When you are His, adopted into the family of God, you carry all the benefits. What's His is yours. The glorious eternity and inheritance are yours. God sees you through the lens of His perfect Son and wants you to share in His good things!

For Reflection: How do you view your heavenly Father? Take some time to pray through your misunderstandings or projections and replace them with truth!

For Meditation: Psalm 23

To Pray: *Lord, I am so thankful that regardless of the earthly examples I've had, You are and will always be my faithful Father. Thank You for drawing me close, loving me, and caring so much about my holiness that You use even my hardships for Your glory. I pray against the false views I have put on You and ask that Your Holy Spirit would replace them with truth. I want to grasp Your true character and love. You are my Good Shepherd and I am so grateful to be Yours. Amen.*

chapter 5

When Waiting Seems Unending: Patience in Christ

Rejoice in hope, be patient in tribulation, be constant in prayer.

ROMANS 12:12 ESV

Something Good Will Grow

As we lean into Christ during our waiting season, patience and His perfect peace will grow in you.

At one point or another in our lives, we have to learn to embrace waiting. While waiting is not my strong suit or anywhere near my top five best attributes, I have seen the Lord hold me miraculously close and download patience in my life during some of the hardest seasons of waiting.

I have learned to sit with the Lord in many seasons of waiting. What are some seasons of difficult waiting you've gone through? As you've probably learned, there are no slick answers that will help us wait, but the good news is that waiting is a practice we learn from personal experience while growing in His grace and patience.

As Oswald Chambers said, "There are not three stages in spiritual life—worship, waiting, and work. Yet some of us seem to jump like spiritual frogs from worship to waiting, and from waiting to work. God's idea is that the three should go together as one. They were always together in the life of our Lord and in perfect harmony. It is a discipline that must be developed; it will not happen overnight."[2] I couldn't agree more. If the opposite of patience can be described as agitated disobedience, then I want to learn how to wait the right way.

Not all waiting is heavy, though. Sometimes it's mundane, like waiting for your gas tank to fill up or for your call to go through or for that website to finally load. As annoying as these things can feel in the moment, they're more of an inconvenience. And some waiting brings happiness: waiting for the proposal, for the baby to be born, or for a vacation to start. In this chapter, we'll address the *true* suffering that is experienced while waiting when we see no hope, when we have no answers, when we feel helpless, and when we can't hear clearly from the Lord. We'll focus on the painful waiting we experience in our lives that feels like torment.

We will always be waiting for something in life, so the question becomes how do we wait *well*? And how do we offer God our pain and remain hopeful as He replaces it with His patience?

Why Is It Still Raining?

I remember a specific year when my waiting felt unbearable. I had recently had blood work and a neck scan and I was waiting on the results, hoping against a possible cancer recurrence. We were waiting for job clarity and for our house to sell because we would be moving. We were waiting for our kids to get better from seasonal school sickness and for time and space to mend relationships. It seemed as if every day we were waiting for news or answers. It felt unending as we held our breath and kept going. Some days, a routine was the only thing that kept me above water. Distraction and routine, rinse and repeat.

This specific year had me waiting in unfamiliar territory and forced me to rely on God in new ways. I learned to sit with Him and to linger in His presence. I couldn't rush my test results, force healthy relationships, or make house buyers appear at the door. I couldn't insert myself into my husband's job negotiations and I couldn't protect my kids from illnesses going around at school. I couldn't be everything to everyone. In fact, I was essentially powerless in all of it. The only option was either to complain (which unfortunately I did at first) or pray for the patience that only the Spirit gives when we choose to seek His presence.

Patience is when we accept the wait. We don't get angry, we don't force circumstances to change, and we don't get agitated. We accept that God is over all, and perfectly sovereign in the waiting. This is easy enough to write, but harder to apply to life situations.

"It's still raining, sweetie, because something still has to grow."

I was driving in the rain to pick up my boys from school and Maddie, our youngest and only girl, started singing in the back seat. "Rain, rain, go away. Come again another day. Little Maddie wants to play. Rain, rain, go away." She looked outside, tracing the droplets on the rainy glass window with a frown on her face and asked, "Why is it still raining?" As if her sweet song could change the weather.

Then she asked me again, "Mama, why is it still raining?"

I felt her innocent question hit my soul because it became personal. I had been asking similar questions of the Lord lately. My heart silently asked, *Why is it still raining, Lord? Have You forgotten us? Do You hear our prayers? Will You come through?*

I was becoming restless with my circumstances, not waiting on the Lord for His plan to prevail or trusting that He knew what He was doing.

Maddie persisted with the question, and asked again, "Mama, why is it still raining? I want to play!"

Then I heard myself responding to her and said, "It's still raining, sweetie, because something still has to grow."

As my eyes filled with tears, I knew at that very moment I would revisit this simple reminder. *I'm still waiting and it's still raining because something still has to grow.* Our season was filled with too much rain, too much waiting, and seemingly too much silence from the Lord.

I'm sure you've experienced times like these. It can feel so isolating and frustrating and painful, but I'll tell you what I also told myself: God is growing you even in this season of unanswered prayers and unending waiting. He's not done with your story. He's not far off. He's *not* ignoring you. Something good is growing while you wait. God is producing something good in your life because of this season, even when the waiting feels unbearable.

Alan Redpath beautifully said, "God will never plant the seed of His life upon the soil of a hard, unbroken spirit. He will only plant that seed where the conviction of His Spirit has brought brokenness, where the soil has been watered with the tears of repentance as well as the tears of joy."[3]

Our seasons of waiting can easily produce bitterness, unhealthy distraction, or anger toward God. We must be wary of our attitude and heart motives going in a negative direction for too long in our waiting. But if we allow our lives to be offerings to Him even when we don't see a way through the storm or spot clear answers, His peace will come when we learn to patiently wait.

When we then see our shortcomings and need for a Savior . . . that is the humble soil the Lord can work with. Our lives can be filled with repentance and conviction, waiting and suffering, often feeling broken, but the joy and beauty that comes after the waiting will transform our angst to a newfound peace that only comes from our generous Father who wants to see us grow, and grow something good.

Living in Both Places

Can you think of a time when you've been refined through waiting? We often ask God to make us more like Christ, but then when the Lord gives us the opportunity to learn through patience, it's quite difficult to flex those muscles when we're not familiar with using them.

From personal experience, I rarely see the reason for my suffering when I am in the middle of it. Many times, it's not until *after* the trial is over that I can look back and see how God grew me in patience no matter my circumstances. Thankfully, the Bible is filled with examples of waiting.

As you read these verses, circle what the writer of each verse is waiting for. Then underline *God* or the *Lord* every time you come to it as a reminder of who we are truly waiting on.

- I waited patiently for the Lord to help me. (Ps. 40:1)
- Let all that I am wait quietly before God, for my hope is in him. (Ps. 62:5)
- I am exhausted from crying for help; my throat is parched. My eyes are swollen with weeping, waiting for my God to help me. (Ps. 69:3)
- So the Lord must wait for you to come to him so he can show you his love and compassion. For the Lord is a faithful God. Blessed are those who wait for his help. (Isa. 30:18)
- As for me, I look to the Lord for help. I wait confidently for God to save me, and my God will certainly hear me. (Micah 7:7)

And my personal favorite: "Yet what we suffer now is nothing compared to the glory he will reveal to us later. For all creations is waiting eagerly for that future day when God will reveal who his children really are" (Rom. 8:18–19).

We can live in both places. Our eyes swollen from tears, throat parched, but also confident that God will save us.

These verses show us the shared difficulty we all have in waiting but also the learned hope, patience, and confidence that comes with practice. We are reminded that our hope is in Him alone, He is a faithful God, we are blessed when we wait for His help, He is waiting for us to come to Him, we can stand in confidence knowing God will save us and hear us, and that ultimately, nothing here on earth compares to what is ahead—a glorious eternity.

If we are His, then our waiting will not be wasted. Waiting patiently turns our focus off our circumstances and onto the throne as we gaze on the One who knows.

As the above verses reveal, we can live in both places. Our eyes swollen from tears, throat parched, but also confident that God will save us. Quieting our hearts, walking through suffering, but also placing our hope in Him. Waiting is to look forward expectantly. Expectantly can mean that you are hopeful, maybe anxious, or even excited, but when you stand on these truths, patience will follow. They won't always bring answers and perfection, but as we continue to grow in patience, we will then receive His perfect peace as we wait on Him, the God who knows all, who sees us, and hears our prayers.

How Long, O Lord?

Looking back on that year, I found myself praying more than I ever have. I also found myself in Psalm 13 a lot.

"How long, LORD? Will you forget me forever? How long will you hide your face from me? How long must I wrestle with my thoughts and day after day have sorrow in my heart? How long will my enemy triumph over me? Look on me and answer, LORD my God" (vv. 1–3 NIV).

We can go to the Father as David did. We can come to the Lord with all of our praise, requests, honor, thanks, and yes, even authentic laments. But just like David, we don't stay there in our complaints and anger. David goes on:

"But I trust in your unfailing love; my heart rejoices in your salvation. I will sing the LORD's praise, for he has been good to me" (vv. 5–6).

David has a heartfelt and honest prayer to God. But then he ends with truth. "I trust in your unfailing love. . . . for he has been good to me." Knowing that I can pray honest prayers while also trusting in God's faithfulness, His plan for my life, and His love for me helps me wait with patience and my heart becomes at peace. He knows your future and what will happen in every situation. You just have to get to a place where you don't have to know the answers and can rest that He knows. *We don't have to know.* He is God, we are not. His plans are better. (We should repeat that to ourselves every day!)

Psalm 13 is a great place to start in your waiting season as it reminds us that we can be honest with the Lord and go to Him in every circumstance and with every one of our emotions. I also find great strength in James 1:2–4:

> When troubles of any kind come your way, consider it an opportunity for great joy. For you know that when your faith is tested, your endurance has a chance to grow. So let it grow, for when your endurance is fully developed, you will be perfect and complete, needing nothing.

So let it grow. Growing takes time. We need to remember in the middle of a trial, there is opportunity for great joy if we allow the Lord to develop us. "I planted the seed in your hearts, and Apollos watered it, but it was God who made it grow. It's not important who does the planting, or who does the watering. What's important is that God makes the seed grow" (1 Cor. 3:5–7).

Nothing happens overnight, and we can't grow in our own strength or find the patience in ourselves to wait *the right and holy way*. It's the trials that produce a patient endurance in us that helps us keep going in life, no matter the circumstance. Next time you find yourself struggling to patiently wait, go back to 1 Corinthians 3 and repeat to yourself, "God makes the seed grow." His timing and ways are perfect.

When we are honest in our prayers and humbling ourselves in trials, authentic patience in the Lord will follow.

I know waiting feels like a place of unending sorrows and hardships, with maybe only a little joy sprinkled in. It can feel like the pain of waiting will outweigh the opportunity to learn patience and receive His peace. But when you have the option to trust His good plan or to complain, you'll find that trusting is the only meaningful option that will carry you through. When you choose trust over and over again, you'll see how endurance is finally produced and His peace is given through your waiting.

Not Forgotten

Sometimes when our waiting seems unending, it can feel like we're forgotten by God. You can do all the things you know you should: pray, read, journal, and find joy, but you still feel lost because God hasn't changed your circumstances, given you answers, or given you the hope you need to keep waiting.

If you truly believe that God has forgotten you, then you don't understand the God who created you and loves you. He's not forgetful.

We know God cares and is over all, but when we look at the unknown with our questions and fears, unrevealed plans and unanswered prayers, it's easy to think that God must not care. He must be busy. We must be doing something wrong. We must try harder or pray more. More distractions. More trying. That's where our hearts can go when the waiting goes on and on.

May I be honest? That's not His character. God's not holding out on you. When you think God will answer deep longings, prayers, and questions for other people but you don't believe it to be true in your own life, then you have placed the Lord in a box. Your firm foundation of knowing God is not as firm as you had hoped.

Read over this passage (Rom. 8:35, 37). You might even substitute your own situation for "trouble or calamity."

> Can anything ever separate us from Christ's love? Does it mean he no longer loves us if we have trouble or calamity, or are persecuted, or hungry, or destitute, or in danger, or threatened with death? . . . No, despite all these things, overwhelming victory is ours through Christ, who loved us.

Does it mean He no longer loves us, or has forgotten us if we have fears or questions or hardships or pain or needs in the middle of waiting? No. He loves us immensely and wants us to come to Him no matter what. If you need something, ask for it. If you have a question, ask it. If you have fears, express them. While you're waiting for answers, He is waiting for you to come to Him in authenticity.

While you feel forgotten, your mature faith should be able to withstand seasons of waiting. God is waiting with open arms. Believe that. He might not answer you in the way you thought was best for your life, but He will answer. I can attest to that, as can countless others. I didn't pray and journal and sign up for a Bible study and then get a perfect health diagnosis or a perfect house or see my troubles turned to miracles the next day. If that's how God worked, we wouldn't need a life of refinement and sanctification.

But we have to remember He cares about us and even cares about the details. We have to remember His love for us and that He wants good things for us. Then, when we finally get to a place of peace through learned experiences of waiting, we trust in His revealed plan and His answers going forward.

Is This the Plan?

When you're feeling forgotten, the story of the healing of Jairus' daughter is a good one to read. Put yourself in Jairus' shoes. Passages in this section are quoted from the English Standard Version.

> When he [Jairus] saw Jesus, he fell at his feet, pleading fervently with him. "My little daughter is dying," he said. "Please come and lay your hands on her; heal her so she can live." (Mark 5:22–23)

As a mom of four children, I can feel Jairus' desperation as I read this. He wanted to see his precious daughter healed, and he knew that Jesus was the only one who could do such a miracle.

> Jesus went with him, and all the people followed. (v. 24)

But then, an interruption. As Jesus was walking with Jairus back to his house, a woman touched His robe. He "realized at once that healing power had gone out of him" and He stopped.

> He turned around in the crowd and asked, "Who touched my robe?" (v. 30)

Pause. If I were Jairus, I'd be thinking, *Okay Jesus, I came to You first; let's get going because my daughter needs You right this second.*

This woman had been overcome with a bleeding disorder, and when she touched the hem of His garment, she was instantly healed. She was "trembling at the realization of what had happened to her" (v. 32). She confessed that she was the one who had touched Jesus' robe.

Jesus told her, "Daughter, your faith has made you well," and encouraged her to "go in peace" because "your suffering is over" (v. 34).

This account is a pleasing interlude, but Jairus may have been getting impatient at the intrusion, expecting Jesus to hurry to *his* house and heal *his* daughter.

We don't know what Jairus was thinking or saying during Jesus' encounter with the bleeding woman, but while Jesus was speaking to her, "messengers arrived from the home of Jairus. They told him, 'Your daughter is dead.' There's no use troubling the Teacher now" (v. 35).

Can you imagine how Jairus felt? An interruption while Jesus healed someone else, and then thinking your chance for a miracle had passed? Your waiting and watching felt pointless. You felt forgotten, your hope and desperation misplaced.

I love that Jesus overheard the messengers speaking to Jairus and said to him, "Don't be afraid. Just have faith" (v. 36). Jairus needed Jesus' soft words in that very moment. The story goes on to tell us that Jesus miraculously healed Jairus' daughter and all was well. There were enough miracles to go around.

Have faith and patience in the waiting because God knows. *Don't be afraid. Just have faith.* We can have peace in the waiting and not fear how things are going to turn out. God knows what He is doing. Even though our minds run at a million miles per second thinking of the worst-case scenarios, what we could have done differently, or what will happen, God cannot be rushed. He is patient, and He will give us the same patience and perfect peace while we wait on Him. Keep waiting and praying for your miracle, but at the end of the day, we pray, "Let Your will be done, Lord."

A Treasured Gift

If you think about it, every person in your life has had to wait for something. Same goes for every person in the Bible. Abraham waited for God to provide a lamb. Joseph waited for justice. The Israelites in the desert waited for signs to go forth. David waited for peace, and everyone was waiting for the Messiah to come. Mary and Martha waited for Lazarus to walk out of the grave. The disciples waited for Jesus to rise from the dead and then waited for the Holy Spirit to direct their path in sharing the gospel.

Everyone waits, so it helps to know we're not alone in this. But look how much good came from the waiting. It's so encouraging that we can have the same hope that our waiting is not meaningless, but—will we choose to wait well?

We can have hope and peace because we know that the waiting is always worth the hard time because of what God produces.

"Be patient, therefore, brothers, until the coming of the Lord. See how the farmer waits for the precious fruit of the earth being patient about it, until it receives the early and late rains. You also, be patient. Establish your hearts, for the coming of the Lord is at hand" (James 5:7–8 ESV).

Our learned patience through waiting will become such a treasured gift when we apply it to the coming King. As we eagerly await Jesus' return, He can turn our unending waiting to a patient hope as we become women of peace.

We can have hope and peace because we know that the waiting is always worth the hard time because of what God produces. And not only do we have a glorious eternity awaiting us, but we have His grace, hope, peace, and patience *today*. Right now.

I know we long for everything in our lives to be wrapped up in a bow every night before we go to sleep, but that's not reality. We have to learn to put all the noise and anxiety and anger aside that waiting ushers in, and walk slow. Intentionally. Recognizing that we don't have all the answers, that we are not forgotten, and that learned patience will carry us through the next season of waiting we have. Something still has to grow. Keep holding on.

Four Habits to Help While We Wait

We can learn so much from waiting, and I believe the more we wait, the more opportunity we have to be filled with peace and hope. Not that all of your burdens will be lifted and questions will be answered if you do this, that, and the other, but there are simple practices that can help. Here are four habits that will encourage you in the midst of waiting.

Cultivate—Work where your feet are planted. Focus on what is right before you. When you are diligent with what you have been given, you'll have less time to focus on the negative aspects of waiting and more time to live out what God is already doing in your life.

Care—Invest in those around you. Love on your kids, friends, family, and neighbors. Put others before yourself. This is one of the best healthy distractions that any of us can have.

Challenge—Give yourself a goal to work toward. Run a mile in a certain amount of time, complete that DIY project you've been putting off, clean your junk drawer, finish the book you started, or journal every morning for five minutes before you start your day. Working toward a challenge and then completing it will give you a sense of purpose while you wait.

Create—Maybe you wouldn't label yourself a creative, but women are natural creators! Bake, write, make content, design, cook a meal, decorate a room, or make up a game for your kids to play. All these get the mind thinking positively and are quite productive during waiting seasons.

If we give the Lord our waiting, He will in turn give us His patience to withstand any circumstance.

Blooming in the Dark

Something Good to Remember: The hard aspects of waiting are always worth it because of the hope and peace that God produces in each season.

For Reflection: Out of the four habits that help in waiting, which can you implement this week? Cultivate, care, challenge, or create?

For Meditation: Psalm 130:5

To Pray: *God, thank You that you are my peace in the waiting. I ask that You remind me of the expectant hope I have in a glorious eternity. Even though I am struggling, I pray that I would feel You close and stand on the truth that I am not forgotten. You hear my prayers, You want what is good for my life, and I am grateful for the learned patience. Go before me this week and help me focus on You in the waiting, not the outcome. Amen.*

chapter 6

When Your Plans Are Derailed: Trust in Christ

"For I know the plans I have for you," declares the LORD, "plans to prosper you and not to harm you, plans to give you a hope and a future. Then you will call on me and come and pray to me, and I will listen to you."

JEREMIAH 29:11–12 NIV

Something Good Will Grow

Every derailed plan brings an opportunity to deepen your trust in God's good plans.

We lost our fourth baby due to miscarriage. It was one of the hardest experiences of my life. When you pray for good things (like children), get pregnant, and then it is taken from you, it sends your spiritual compass spiraling.

Shortly after the loss of our baby, we learned we'd be moving across the country from Colorado to North Carolina for my husband's job. This move meant we'd be away from community, support, church, my parents, and friends. I had thought we'd stay in Colorado forever and I was devastated. Shortly after we found out we'd be moving, I was diagnosed with thyroid cancer.

Talk about plans being derailed! Here I was, expecting that a newborn would soon be added to our family. Nope. I thought we were staying in Colorado. Nope. I thought I was healthy. Nope. These weren't small derailments that set me back a couple of steps. These were major, life-altering happenings that flung me far from where I thought I was headed.

That specific season of my life still defines me and challenges me in many ways. It was one of the hardest times of my life. In the middle of my mess and pain, I couldn't see clearly. I was broken and hard-hearted at times. I couldn't see an end in sight, only my current grief. Fear clouded my judgment. Ultimately this time rocked my foundation of hope that God could do something with all that I was walking through.

I lacked peace. I constantly worried about my kids, wondering if they would be okay as I was going through so much physically, mentally, and spiritually. I also thought I was becoming a burden and felt I was getting in the way of what God was doing in my husband's life and his career. I worried for my own life and health and how I would feel physically going forward.

Derailments sent me to a dark spot.

Whether it's everyday disruptions like a child's attitude or a broken washing machine, or heavy disruptions like a move across the country or health challenges, we all know what it's like to have our plans derailed.

He Is Always Faithful

"But God."

In the midst of the chaos of all my plans being gutted, God faithfully got me and my family through. Over time, He provided people, resources, babysitters, doctors, surgeons, friends, finances, meals . . . everything practical we needed to get through plus more. He comforted me in the process, equipped me, grew me, and strengthened my faith. He took care of me.

But I definitely didn't see all those good things at first. My mind was filled with questions and deep doubts:

Was I dying?

Would we have the help we needed?

Will we ever get pregnant again?

Will my kids be okay?

Will this be too much for my husband, Andrew, to handle as he starts his new position?

Will my body ever heal?

While I can look back *now* and see how He provided every step of the way, it didn't mean this season was easy breezy and that I trusted Him during each aspect of the process. All I saw was hardship, caught in a briar patch of sharp problems with nowhere for me to run. I could struggle and blindly try getting out on my own, only to get cut even deeper. Or I could be obedient, doing my part to trust that God would be faithful to guide me every step. He is *always* faithful.

It's normal to head into disruptions with questions and fears and pain and doubts. But once God gets you through—which He will—it builds your trusting muscles and strengthens your faith to know, really know, that nothing can separate you from the love of God. I held on to this truth and continue to as I walk forward in life. Nothing I go through, not a cancer diagnosis, loss, move across the country, or anything else for that matter, can thwart God's redeeming plan and love for me.

Will we have hardships and cry in the process and grieve and lament and lose sleep and ache with every fiber of our being at times? Absolutely. But we are human, awaiting a glorious eternity and, as we wait, our divine assignment is to trust the Divine.

Walking through this intense season of derailment has helped me trust Him for the "next times." No, I don't trust every time perfectly. But going forward, no matter what comes my way, I *know* He will be faithful and carry me through. Now, every derailment, big or small, provides an opportunity to live out what I have learned to be true.

I can stand on the truth that He will never leave me nor forsake me, that He will use what I walk through for His glory, and that He will equip me to keep going. I know He will provide everything I need, He will take great care of me in the process, and God Himself will be all that I need.

God is worthy of your trust in all seasons, even the ones that make no sense.

Disruptions reveal the heartbeat of your faith. But how do we live this out? We can't just flip a switch and be "fine" in our biggest disappointments. We can't just read a Bible verse and suddenly be okay. And quite frankly, you can't just read this chapter and start trusting. How do we practically live this out?

Trust starts with a single decision: a choice to trust Him.

In his book *Dark Clouds, Deep Mercy,* Mark Vroegop says, "Trust is believing what you know to be true even though the facts of suffering might call that belief into question."[4]

Fact: You will face suffering and heartache.

Fact: Suffering and heartache are agonizing and painful.

Fact: It's human to be shocked and hurt and confused when your plans are disrupted.

But even though we live in a messed-up, evil, and sinful world, God is worthy of your trust in all seasons, even the ones that make no sense.

Trust Is a Process

I didn't trust God immediately when I found out that I had lost a baby; I didn't think all things would work together. I didn't trust God immediately when I heard that we'd be moving across the country; I didn't think that was what was best for our family. I sure didn't trust God immediately when I received a cancer diagnosis. At first, none of it made sense.

My pride and my plans got in the way of my trust . . . at first. Trust doesn't just instantly illuminate our lives like the flick of a light switch. Many times it's a process. Past storms strengthened my trust muscle, making it easier to choose to trust going forward. You may be seasoned in your walk with the Lord and have built those trust muscles over time to where you can stand on Christ, your solid rock, regardless of what comes your way. That's what the testing of our trials do to our faith. Trials give us strength!

Don't just take my word for it. Listen to what God's Word teaches.

> For you know that the testing of your faith produces steadfastness. And let steadfastness have its full effect, that you may be perfect and complete, lacking in nothing. (James 1:3–4 ESV)

You might be walking through your first "big" derailment right now and it's hard to understand God in it. If that's the case for you, may I tell you something as someone who has walked through a lot? God will work out His plans for your life. In fact, I can promise you this. Psalms 138:8 says, "The LORD will work out his plans for my life—for your faithful love, O LORD, endures forever." God is the only one who will bring you through, prove faithful, and never fail you in the middle of your derailment. People won't produce the miracle you're looking for in your hard place. Only God can do that.

Lean In to the Uncomfortable

We love comfort, don't we? But part of trusting God's plan is recognizing that leaning in to His plan and will often brings discomfort to our lives. This is normal. But we are so accustomed to and desirous of living in a pain-free bubble that when we're *not* comfortable, we think we must not be where God wants us to be. We believe He wants us comfortable and living the easy life, so when that's not our reality, we assume we must not be walking in His will.

But—trusting God to direct our paths, even when it's uncomfortable, nerve-racking, or hard is exactly where we should be.

Don't let the fear of discomfort keep you from trusting His plan. You might just miss out on the redemption, beauty, transformation, and precious opportunity to give God glory through your life.

Think of the disciples Jesus chose. When He first saw the two brothers who fished for a living, Simon (Peter) and Andrew, "Jesus called out to them, 'Come, follow me, and I will show you how to fish for people!' And *they left their nets at once* and followed him" (Matt. 4:19–20).

They left their nets at once! I'm assuming that when Simon and Andrew woke up that morning, their plan wasn't to leave the job and work they'd done for years and follow this Jesus. Talk about a disruption! *That is undeniable trust.* I ask myself when I read this, *Would I have done the same*? Would you? There is a commitment and cost to following Christ that means there is an *effort* on our part. A choice. A dying to self. Giving up what's comfortable. Why not embrace the disruption? Instead of resisting, walk the path Jesus has laid out for you. It might even be paved and smoother than you had imagined.

Simon and Andrew knew what you can know. Jesus was their everything, even in deep discomfort.

The thing that's wild to me is that this wasn't just a one-time thing. If you keep going in Matthew 4, we read, "A little farther up the shore he (Jesus) saw two other brothers, James and John, sitting in a boat with their father, Zebedee, repairing their nets. And he called them to come, too. They immediately followed him, leaving the boat and their father behind" (vv. 21–22 NLT).

Immediately. They immediately followed him! This is so convicting for me because I think when our life is too comfortable and we have our own plans and our own lives, we miss out on the calling of Christ. To come to Him. To follow. We forget that our life is not our own and that when our comfort is uprooted by Jesus, our lives begin to bring so much good and depth and glory.

These disciples left their work. They left their comforts. They laid down their plans for the day, and for their lives. They had to surrender their reputations. They had to give up control.

While I know plans being derailed come in all shapes and sizes, the questions we have to ask ourselves are what are we giving up, if anything? And what are we leaving behind to follow Christ?

In the specific instances I was going through and all that came with those painful circumstances, I had to humble myself and give up my own understanding. Even the core of my basic understanding of Christianity was uprooted, so much so, that after the fact, I finally saw trials and suffering in a new light. I don't welcome trials, but I can see the faithfulness of the Lord and how He truly "causes everything to work together for the good of those who love God and are called according to his purpose for them" (Rom. 8:28).

God isn't sitting up in heaven, mustering up the craziest bouts of suffering to completely derail your life so you trust Him. Life just happens to be really awful sometimes. That's the reality of the fallen world we're living in. But because God is good, He's the one who turns disruptions for your good and His glory. I know your life and circumstances can feel like a joke at times, and you might think there's no way to bloom in your current reality. But God is always good and faithful. The waves are crashing over us, the weather feels like a constant pelting of hail, the chaos is undeniable, but this season won't be forever. God is good in the midst of it all. He's the one looking down on you saying, "Let's make something beautiful again from this broken mess." And He is always faithful to do so.

Make a conscious effort to trust God and understand you will be uncomfortable when you follow Him. These are great reminders when your life feels derailed.

Redefining "Good"

In God's Word, you will find many verses about "good things" in our life that come from a faithful God. You may feel encouraged when reading one of these verses after having a bad day, only to realize that God's definition of "good" and our human definition of "good" might not exactly align.

It's important to remember that when we are reading God's Word, we need to read it verse by verse as a whole so that we get the full context and can then exposit it correctly when talking to and teaching others. I'd be doing you a huge disservice if I tell you when you repent and live for Christ, then you will have a perfect and pain-free life because God is good. Yes, God is good, but not in the He-gives-you-whatever-you-want way. A life without disruption is never promised.

Let's go over these four often-quoted verses (all from the New International Version):

- "In all things God works for the *good* of those who love him." (Rom. 8:28)
- "No *good* thing does he withhold from those whose walk is blameless." (Ps. 84:11)
- His "*goodness* and love will follow me all the days of my life." (Ps. 23:6)
- "For I know the plans I have for you," declares the LORD, "plans to prosper you and not to harm you, plans to give you a hope and a future." (Jer. 29:11)

They all sound pretty positive, right? I love these reminders! But what do *good things* actually mean in these verses?

We can read these and think, "I love God, so everything is going to work out how I see fit!" Or, "I'd consider myself righteous, so God is going to give me everything I want!" Or, "His goodness and mercy will follow me forever, so life is going to be filled with health and wealth and prosperity!" Or even, "With God, I will only prosper and I will never be harmed!"

Unfortunately, those are all very me-centered ways to dissect passages of Scripture. The Bible is not primarily a book about us and how we think. The Bible is a book about God, His story of redemption through His Son Jesus Christ, how He thinks, and what He expects of us. I think a lot of us get uncomfortable with the truth of what Scripture can mean because it forces us to take the back seat and submit our life to a holy God we might not fully understand or find hard to trust. We want to believe God will give us whatever we want, not what we need. We want to believe God will do what we pray for, not what He knows is best. We want to believe God will work all things out on our timeline, not truly praying, "Let Your will be done, Lord." We want to believe God will work it all out our way rather than fully submitting to whatever He has planned for us.

We want to believe God will work it all out our way rather than fully submitting to whatever He has planned for us.

I know from my life, *good* can mean spiritual growth. I know *good* can mean learning selflessness, learning forgiveness, having conviction or humility. I know *good* can be growing in character, endurance, and hope as the apostle Paul writes in Romans 5:3–5.

Ultimately, what makes us more like Christ is what is *good.*

And what makes us more like Christ? A lot of times, the testing of our faith, plans derailed, trials. In all things, if we know the God we serve, we know He is worthy of our trust and that His ways are better.

Blessing Outweighs Evil

Go back to the foundation of your faith and remember that your life is not your own. You are an offering to the Lord, and your life is to make . . . who known? Him known. Not yourself. Not your job or your business or your kids or your spouse. It's to make Christ known and bring glory to His name through whatever way He is calling you to. And that can be hard, right? There's something in each of us that crinkles our nose at accepting that life isn't all about us.

But in this truth, we also know that the hard parts of life and the difficult experiences we go through will push us to Jesus. We can either lean into Christ when derailments happen, or we can run. We have free will to choose either option. God promises that all things work together for the good of those who love Him. He says that He will withhold no good thing from the righteous. And His goodness will follow us all of our days.

What does the Lord desire of us? "To do what is right, to love mercy, and to walk humbly with your God" (Micah 6:8). Love Him with all your heart, soul, and strength. Live a life to please Him. Watch for the good gifts from above He has for you (James 1:17). Good things come with obedience and submission to Christ.

The blessing of what God did with my pain far outweighed the evil this world threw at me. The opportunities He created far outweighed the brokenness we experienced.

God's ways are truly best and when you trust Him, you believe that nothing happens outside of His will and understanding. Meaning, He knew I was going to lose a baby and have cancer, but He also knew that I was going to heal over time and have a miracle baby girl a year and a half later! He knew our move from Colorado would be extremely difficult, but He also knew

He'd bless us with fulfilling friendships, a beautiful property, and an incredible job for Andrew in North Carolina. The blessing of what God did with my pain far outweighed the evil this world threw at me. The opportunities He created far outweighed the brokenness we experienced. I see that now! So, if we can understand that's the God we serve, we can get through anything with His strength.

The hard circumstances you're facing right now are not defined as good, but what God will do with it when you're submitted to Him *will* be good. So good! We have the choice to either lean into His grace and trust God in our storm, or to reject His love and goodness and try to make something good grow on our own.

Try a Reset

I'm not a big self-help kind of person because I know it never truly satisfies like I want it to. But as I journal in my seasons of derailment and I'm having a hard time trusting, I do a RESET. It truly helps me refocus my eyes on the only One who is worthy of our trust.

Rest
Embrace the Hard
Surround Yourself
Exert Energy
Talk to God

Rest

We'll talk more about rest in another chapter, but I noticed in my difficult season that I was wired with worry. This caused lack of sleep and a restlessness that brought anxiety. May I encourage you to rest in this season right now? Take a nap. Close your eyes. Let His peace wash over you. Sit on your porch and listen to the birds. Take a rest from your to-do list or social media. Resting brings realignment as you pause and listen to what God is saying. What "rest" works for you?

Embrace the Hard

Recognize that this season might just be awful. You can be honest and say it's miserable. Grieve. Lament. Question. But always start with God and if you waver, always go back to Him.

Surround Yourself

Surround yourself with Scripture and sound wisdom. Ground yourself. Derailments are not a time for folly or letting yourself be swayed in the wind like a tumbleweed. This season needs your discipline. Make sure you have people speaking truth into your life and encouraging you. Be in the Word. A lot of times we like to get off track because it's easier and more comfortable to shove away our pain and pretend it's not there. This will never take you where you need to be.

Exert Energy

Go on a daily walk alone or with a friend. Start working out. Be on top of your cleaning. We don't need to stay busy for the sake of being busy, but there is a line between needed rest and laziness. Get some sun on your face, work in your garden, take your dog for a walk, or start a project. Your heart pumping will help with the angst your soul feels during a season of shifting waters.

Talk to God

Don't ever stop your conversations with the Lord. In all times, in all feelings, in all hardships, go to the Lord. He's not scared of you and He's not surprised by your feelings. He wants you to come to Him because He knows He's the best One to walk you through. He loves you and wants good things for you!

Trust and Obey

Sometimes I just pray, "Help me trust You, Lord!" I know in all things that I even need God to help me in my times of doubt and confusion (see Mark 9:24). A. W. Tozer said it this way in *The Root of the Righteous*: "It is altogether doubtful whether any man can be saved who comes to Christ for His help but with no intention to obey Him. Christ's savior-hood is forever united to His Lordship."[5] This is a piercing statement worth reading over a couple of times!

Here's a bottom-line question: Will you honor God when your life is not going as you had planned? Often, our pride trumps our humility. We initially trust God because we know He helps, and will save us eternally. But we may forget the aspect of obeying Him in daily life. Obedience requires trust. We must get to a place where we are living out both. The more disruptions to your life, the more you have the opportunity to trust and obey. Will you do it perfectly every time? No. But as every derailment comes, you will continue to develop until one day I believe that no matter what comes your way, you will boldly say in the words of the hymn, "It is well with my soul."

We don't hold on for what we can get out of God. We hold on because we trust in His goodness.

It is well with my soul. I close my eyes and feel a soft breeze on my face. I hear sounds of the farm, the wind chime clinking, birds calling, church bells in the distance, and best of all, laughing kids as their growing bare feet run through the grass. Who knew this farm in North Carolina and four kids is where God would guide me? I would have never imagined this life while I was lying in a hospital bed after the oncologist had removed the cancer from my body and wishing I was with Jesus instead. I would have never doubted God's plan if He showed me what I have now. I would have never questioned if I knew what God would do years later.

But that's the thing. We don't hold on for what we can get out of God. We hold on because we trust in His goodness. We don't have a blind faith because we know the One guiding us. We know His character and His faithfulness that stands against any hardship.

If you get anything out of this chapter, know that your act of obedience by trusting in His plan and His ways will be the best learned habit to carry you through the rest of your life.

Blooming in the Dark

Something Good to Remember: When my plans are disrupted I have one choice to make: Will I trust God's goodness?

For Reflection: Do you believe God's ways are the best ways? If not, what is keeping you from believing His trustworthy character?

For Meditation: Romans 8:28

To Pray: *God, I am so grateful for You. I'm grateful for what You've done and for how You are worthy of my trust. Through all of the disappointments and derailments that I have faced and am facing now, help me believe that Your ways are the best ways! Help me cling to You and Your Word when everything around me is a mess. I need You. Thank You for always proving faithful, and even when my circumstances are confusing, help me rest in Your trustworthy and faithful character. I know You love me and want good things for me! Amen.*

chapter 7

When the Wound Doesn't Close: Longsuffering in Christ

Even though the fig trees have no blossoms, and there are no grapes on the vines; even though the olive crop fails, and the fields lie empty and barren; even though the flocks die in the fields, and the cattle barns are empty, yet I will rejoice in the LORD! I will be joyful in the God of my salvation! The Sovereign LORD is my strength!

HABAKKUK 3:17–19

Something Good Will Grow

When the wound doesn't close, we develop roots beneath the surface as we learn the valuable skill of endurance.

If you're an avid hiker, you may have heard about the Incline in Manitou Springs, Colorado. With over 2,700 steps rising over 2,000 feet in elevation, this uphill hike is much more difficult than its length of just under a mile would suggest.

The first time I ever climbed the Incline almost two decades ago, I started off strong. I was athletic and lean, and walking up some stairs sounded easy. I had my pump-up music on, my water bottle was full, and I was cruising.

But within fifteen minutes, I was exhausted. Just as I was feeling the burn, thinking about going slower or taking a break, I looked up and saw what I thought was the top. There it was: the summit! The end was within reach; *just push a little more, I'm going to make it!*

That's when another hiker told me something that burst my bubble. He probably saw my excitement as I geared up for the last stretch.

He looked at me, pointed upward and said, "That's the *false* summit right there. The Incline continues for about another thousand steps after that. But keep going! You're halfway there!"

I honestly don't know how I finally made it to the top because I was so discouraged, and dreading the rest of the climb. I started questioning if making it to the top would even be worth it and thought *maybe the view isn't that great.* I had used up almost all my energy just to get to that point. I didn't want to go all the way back down, and I couldn't just give up and sit on a step forever. *I had to have the hope of what was to come.* I had to keep climbing. My legs felt like Jello. My shirt was soaking wet with sweat. My face was strawberry red, and my iPod was out of battery.

But I did it, and now I can tell you that when you finally reach the summit, you'll find a huge sense of accomplishment that overrides your sore muscles or aching journey that got you there. The pain is worth it just for that feeling of success. Plus, the view *is* incredible.

While a climb up a mountain may be a cakewalk compared to the difficulties and devastations we'll face in life, the principles of hope and endurance that are built because of longsuffering are the same.

> Therefore do not throw away your confidence, which has a great reward. For you have need of endurance, so that when you have done the will of God you may receive what is promised.
> (Heb. 10:35–36 ESV)

God is lovingly reminding you that even though the climb is more than hard, even though there are deep sorrows, and even though the suffering in your life continues, He is using everything you go through to make you more like Christ. You can rejoice knowing that the difficulties you face are not meaningless.

You may feel like you're halfway up the mountain right now. Staring up ahead, hopeless, looking around for help, and thinking there is no way you're going to have enough endurance to make it. The pain is too much to handle and the heaviness of life weighs you down.

You keep seeing the false summit and think you can't keep going. *I want to give up. Nothing good is going to come from this longsuffering.*

You're Not Alone

You planted a precious seed of faithfulness and fortitude in hopes of beautiful things happening, and yet, the seed failed, withered, and never bloomed. Nothing grew, only something learned. This chapter is for you if you're asking:

What happens when God doesn't bring resolution?

What will I do if He doesn't heal me?

What happens when there is no good I can see?

What happens when God hasn't fixed my relationship or changed my circumstance?

What happens when there is no reconciliation or no miracle?

There seems to be no hope right now and nothing "working for your good." You're feeling purposeless, defeated, and weary. Your pain has continued for years and years (and years).

A lot about what I've written in this book as I share my life with you has happened in the past. But even as I'm writing these words right now, some heavy and damaging situations are going on that have continued for years. I see no resolution. I've wept as I write and things have flared up and I think, *Nothing is ever going to grow in my life from such a place of heartache.*

I lost hope. Again.

This pain we feel in times like these is not a one-and-done type of pain. It doesn't always mend simply by the passage of time. It isn't the type of pain that happens, you get counseling, work through it, and then it's over. This isn't even the type of pain that leaves a small scar on your body.

The type of pain that we're talking about in this chapter is the gaping, open wounds in our lives, wounds that won't close.

The type of pain we're talking about in this chapter is the gaping, open wounds in our lives, wounds that won't close. It's not that God doesn't care. It's just that His will is to keep them open in your life right now. And that truth hurts us even more because we just want the miracle . . . now. We just want the prayer answered . . . today. We just want reconciliation or answers and we feel as if our souls can't rest until there is a resolution.

We sit up, night after night, begging God to show up in the way we think is best. And time and time again, we don't understand why God is doing what He's doing (or really not doing). We start to have moments of doubt in our faith. We get up the next morning uninterested in prayer, but we try to pray and hope again: "Today is the day that God will move!" But time and time again, it's not in the way we thought, or seemingly at all.

If you know the weight of longsuffering, I will say it again. This chapter is for you if:

You fear your situation will never be healed in the way you think it will be . . .

Your wounds are not only open, but they may never close on this side of eternity . . .

Your view of God wavers because you're tempted every day to give up . . .

You're not alone.

I believe we're learning the most transformative and important skill right now through our pain, without even knowing it: endurance.

Sharing in Christ's Suffering

When suffering becomes longsuffering, platitudes lose their meaning. You believe God is good, but that statement doesn't remove all the ache in your heart. You trust Jesus to take the wheel, but if you hear that song one more time, you're going to go crazy. You know God is a miracle worker, but the span of years this suffering has lasted drives you to stop asking. You just want strength to get through today.

I've walked through suffering, and I'm walking through longsuffering. They aren't the same.

Longsuffering is actually a fruit of the Spirit. But if you read the list in Galatians 5:22–23, you'll see that patience or forbearance is usually listed instead of "longsuffering," as the term is rendered in the King James Version (and the New KJV). I found this interesting because it's so easy to read, "love, joy, peace, patience, kindness, goodness, faithfulness, gentleness, and self-control" and think we have it all together when it comes to patience. We pray for deeper and more lasting patience, of course, but if we're honest, patience in everyday life feels like a choice any person, even a four-year-old in line at Disney, can make.

But longsuffering? We don't pray for longsuffering and we *need* the Holy Spirit for that. Longsuffering is grown over time and learned through sufferings. It is not something the bystander of this world would sign up for, which proves the Holy Spirit is the only one who can help.

When the notes and cards fizzle out and you have to wake up yet another morning and do it all over again, something good is growing.

Suffering is the pain, hurt, distress, and hardships we face with an end in sight, but longsuffering is drawn-out agony, often ascribed to relational suffering. The child's health that is an unending battle, the sick parent you're praying God will take to heaven and release from years of anguish, the wayward child you're trusting to Christ but seeing no change in, or the relationship that keeps burdening you with their problems.

It's prolonged pain that you have a choice to bear with patient endurance. When the "how are you" questions stop coming, the meal train ends, the notes and cards fizzle out, and you have to wake up yet another morning and do it all over again, something good is growing. You are learning to endure. Longsuffering is suffering drawn out, continuous, with seemingly no answers. But as awful as it is and as it sounds, not much is more important to learn as a follower of Christ. When we long suffer, we suffer as Christ suffered.

> And since we are his children, we are his heirs. In fact, together with Christ we are heirs of God's glory. But if we are to share his glory, we must also share his suffering. (Rom. 8:17)

When you are in a family, you endure hardships together. My journey through cancer affected our entire household. Thankfully, my boys were too little at the time to fully understand, but I know it was extremely difficult for Andrew and also for the kids in their own way. When something or someone hurts one of the family members, it hurts everyone.

On the flip side, we also share in the family blessings. Andrew is an extremely hard worker, and when he gets a bonus or we save over time, the kids get the benefit of a fun vacation or an addition to the farm. We share in one another's blessings by being included in a family.

As Christians in the family of God, we will reap the benefits and share in the sorrows. If we are now co-heirs with Christ (Rom. 8:17), we share in His blessings and glory. We are now filled with the Holy Spirit, and can cling to hope in every season. But we also share in His sufferings as we face horrible days, devastating circumstances, and experience the evils of this world while living for His name's sake.

We will suffer, be persecuted, slandered, and broken. We share those sufferings with Christ as He lived thirty-three years in this world and went to the cross once and for all to save our souls for eternity. Jesus might not have walked exactly what you're walking, but He *understands* because He bore it all on the cross.

Isaiah 53:4 says, "It was our weaknesses he carried; it was our sorrows that weighed him down."

Hope in Both

Growing up, I always heard the positive stories. Noah saving his family and being obedient even when others laughed and didn't believe him. David as the little guy who won out over the giant. I heard about Job receiving more blessings in the latter days of his life than his beginning (what some call the "double portion"), the courage of Esther, and Lazarus walking out of the grave. I heard about Abraham and Sarah's promised child and about the miracles of the New Testament.

But there is more to the story. The Bible isn't just about happy earthly endings. It is a profound disservice to others if we teach only the good. When you only hear stories of prayers answered, promises fulfilled, and miracles happening, it's no wonder so many believe that after short hardships, we're all just going to receive our double portion on earth like Job, or our miracle child, like Abraham and

Sarah. It's no wonder we believe that if we do x, y, and z in our faith, then we'll receive what we think we deserve. We're missing the fruit of longsuffering, the reward of courage, the benefits of denying yourself, and the peace that only comes through surrender.

While those stories are encouraging and hopeful, they also have a lot of hardships woven into their joys. Job still lost ten children and all of his earthly possessions. Abraham and Sarah still had difficulty because of their lack of trust in God's plan, resulting in bringing in Hagar, and later the turmoil leading up to Abraham believing he would sacrifice Isaac. We also know David committed many sins and lost a newborn, as well as his son Absalom as an adult. While those were their personal stories, we can see both joy and pain in them all.

Some wounds will probably not close on this side of heaven.

I can tell you after walking through all that I have, some wounds will probably not close on this side of heaven. You might not get your double portion or your miracle until you are face-to-face with Jesus. You might not be raised up in this life and you might not see the impact of your ministry. You might not see your prayer answered (in the way you think is best) or the restoration you long for. You are not a clone of Job or Sarah or Esther or any of these Bible characters. You are unique and God is doing a *new thing in you.*

A life of suffering is not a maybe. It's a promise. A life of perfection and happy endings is not.

> In this world, you will have tribulation . . . John 16:33
> If you want to live a godly life, you will suffer . . . 2 Timothy 3:12
> Don't be surprised when trials come . . . 1 Peter 4:12
> Your faith will be tested . . . James 1:2–4
> You will suffer awhile . . . 1 Peter 5:10

Our happy ending will always remain in Christ alone. Glory with Him *is* our happy ending!

My convictions are too deep, and I cannot sit here and type these words and tell you that as a Christian "everything will work out for you" *in the way you see fit and the way you think is best.* Does God have you? Absolutely. Do we live in a fallen world? Yes. Is our hope on earth or our circumstances? No, our hope is in Jesus. We must know what the Bible teaches about suffering on earth or else you'll think that God only gets the glory when your life is going well and that God is only good when you get your miracle.

We must know what the Bible teaches about suffering on earth or else you'll think God is only good when you get your miracle.

Don't forget about Moses and David. Moses learned endurance as he faced Pharaoh over and over again and then wandered in the desert for forty years. He needed to draw from that learned endurance to complete his God-given assignment, even though he would not receive or see the full reward on earth. David learned endurance as he went from shepherd boy to defeating Goliath and then to be anointed king. He needed to draw from that learned endurance to live out God's plan for the Israelites.

There are many other examples of people in the Bible having to learn endurance. The question becomes, do we trust that God is sovereign, and do we trust God with our lives?

Because what happens when God does get the most glory from your life by *not* healing you? What happens when God receives the most glory out of your life through an *unresolved* relationship? What happens when God receives the most glory in your *difficult* circumstance? What happens when a nonbelieving friend looks at you and marvels at your ability to endure with joy? What happens is that they want what you have. You were laid off at work, yet still radiate the joy of the Lord because you trust in Him. Your life becomes the greatest witness.

Choosing Christ

The prophet Habakkuk wrote these powerful words about long-suffering:

> Even though the fig trees have no blossoms, and there are no grapes on the vines; even though the olive crop fails, and the fields lie empty and barren; even though the flocks die in the fields, and the cattle barns are empty, yet I will rejoice in the LORD! I will be joyful in the God of my salvation! The Sovereign LORD is my strength! (Hab. 3:17–19)

I have to ask myself if I approach longsuffering as Habakkuk did. If there is no resolution, no miracle, no answers, do I still choose Christ? Do I still rejoice because God is my salvation and my hope is heavenward?

I've even had to ask similar questions in the past.

If I'm not healed of cancer . . .
If I got pregnant from rape . . .
If the depression doesn't go away . . .
If the slander continues . . .

Habakkuk was reminding himself, and through the inspired Word he is reminding us, that regardless of our earthly circumstances, we can have hope, not only in what is to come from glory forever, but that we have Christ *now*. We have salvation *now*. Your faithfulness can't be determined by your circumstances because God's faithfulness isn't determined by your circumstances. He is unchanging.

In fact, we read in Hebrews 11 about the great faith and endurance of Abel (v. 4), Enoch (v. 5), Noah (v .7), Abraham (v. 8), and many others. "Faith shows the reality of what we hope for; it is the evidence of things we cannot see" (v. 1). We don't have to cross our fingers, hoping for a glorious eternity with our Lord. We can have the assurance of our salvation while also remembering the many others who went before us in faith and didn't live a life of perfection either.

Our hearts should be set on heaven, longing for what's ahead, because our life here is but a breath compared to an eternity with the Father.

> All these people died still believing what God had promised them. *They did not receive what was promised, but they saw it all from a distance and welcomed it.* They agreed that they were foreigners and nomads here on earth. Obviously people who say such things are looking forward to a country they can call their own. If they had longed for a country they came from, they could have gone back. But they were looking for a better place, a heavenly homeland. That is why God is not ashamed to be called their God, for he has prepared a city for them. (Heb. 11:13–16)

In other words, sometimes we see the outcome and rewards of our faith here on earth. Sometimes we do not. But it's not about what our endurance can get us at the end of our life. It's about how God uses our learned endurance to suffer well and fulfill our purpose here. Our hearts should be set on heaven, longing for what's ahead, because our life here is but a breath compared to an eternity with the Father. Heaven is our true home and we are foreigners here. I think if we all endured and got our happy endings and resolutions here on earth, we wouldn't crave heaven as we do with trials and heartache. Suffering reminds us of what is to come as we share in His sufferings and glory.

The Promise

Proverbs 4:25–26 (NIV) says, "Let your eyes look straight ahead; fix your gaze directly before you. Give careful thought to the paths for your feet and be steadfast in all your ways." When you surrender to Christ, stand on His truth, and let Him work in and through you, even in your longsuffering, you will be equipped for whatever comes your way. As you suffer, God is teaching you to endure. Let's remind ourselves of what is true:

> We have questions, but we won't lose hope.
>
> We are exhausted from life, but we will remain faithful.
>
> We commit to embracing the sanctifying work of suffering in our lives.
>
> We are learning to endure.

You don't have to endure forever, just until glory. This too shall pass, because the heavens and earth are passing away.

There is deep, sanctifying heart work happening in your life that is unseen. The most important part of any plant and flower is its unseen roots. The same goes for you and me. No matter what danger or weather may come above ground, if your roots are deep, you will remain. You will be able to endure whatever comes your way because your roots are intertwined in Christ. While roots aren't pretty and no one is picking them and putting them on the kitchen table in a vase, they are a vital component of every thriving plant.

In longsuffering, we don't focus on what will grow, worrying about the bloom that will come. We focus on our foundation in Christ, allowing Him to do the sanctifying work of molding deep roots in us, so that we can endure in all things.

Blooming in the Dark

Something Good to Remember: Our promise isn't in suffering going away, it's in Christ Himself, the hope of glory.

For Reflection: If you're walking through longsuffering, what verse can you cling to this coming week? Write it on a note card and memorize it because the Word is what will help you endure.

For Meditation: Hebrews 11:13

To Pray: *Lord, thank You for being my sustaining grace. Thank You that I get to share in Your glory and in Your sufferings as a child in Your family. I pray that You would continue to give me the patience to endure in my longsuffering and the hope of what is to come. Amen.*

chapter 8

When Your Health Falters: Strength in Christ

Our bodies are buried in brokenness, but they will be raised in glory. They are buried in weakness, but they will be raised in strength.

1 CORINTHIANS 15:43

Something Good Will Grow

As our bodies fail, our souls are sanctified in strength!

Having cancer ushers in a slew of new routines, which may include gluten-free eating, medication for life, biopsies, scans, and blood work.

Maybe you too understand the struggles of a life with health challenges. Whether you're dealing with aging, a diagnosis or disease, fluctuating hormones, or pregnancy and childbirth, we all long to be free from the effects of the fall on our bodies.

Before I was diagnosed with cancer, I didn't go to the doctor much and rarely worried about my health. For all I knew, I was a healthy mom with three healthy boys under the age of four. Of course, I was exhausted from motherhood and having a husband who was often away from home as he pursued his medical degree, but I just chalked it up to a normal, busy, full season of life.

Then the miscarriage happened, and shortly afterward I heard these words: "You have cancer."

To be so young with cancer, only thirty years old at the time, felt extremely daunting. All of a sudden, there was a Nicole before cancer, and a Nicole after cancer.

Before I go on, I want you to know that I understand what it feels like to be lying in a hospital bed thinking this is where your story ends.

I know what it feels like to have your anxiety flare up before you go to a yearly checkup that could determine the rest of your life.

Faltering health has changed me in some of the worst ways but has mostly changed me in the best ways.

I know what it feels like to have your body be poked and prodded and bruised from so many labs and tests.

I know what it feels like to manage medication that you need to survive, only to find out that you feel different every month depending on the dosage.

I know what it feels like to have a body so sensitive to change that you feel defeated because it might never get better.

I know what it feels like to have hormonal changes, to birth babies, not appreciating what is reflected in the mirror, and feeling like an eighty-year-old trapped in a body half that age.

I know I might be considered young as I write this, but when it comes to health, I can relate to just about any woman reading these words.

My health faltering and failing me has changed me. It's changed me in some of the worst ways as I have become more pessimistic and fatigued, but cancer has mostly changed me in the best ways. The Lord used cancer in my life to humble me and heal me in ways that I probably wouldn't have learned if it weren't for that diagnosis.

Lessons in Weakness

One of the most important lessons I learned through cancer was that I had to rely on others. Cancer forced me to face that I'm not superwoman. I was forced to take the back seat and become a listener, not a doer. I had to learn patience in the healing process as I waited for results and treatment.

The standards I have for myself will always be high, but I'm living more in the valley of grace since walking through cancer. I sympathize with the sick and have more of a heart for those suffering through daily health challenges. I was knocked off my high horse and brought to my knees before the throne. I was forced to face the reality that I'm not in control of my life. I finally saw my life as it really is—in the hands of a faithful God.

What I gained from cancer was far more than I lost. What God produced was more than He pruned. Cancer grew me up spiritually and helped me see my life through a different lens. I saw how fleeting life is, how important my husband and kids are to me, and how even in my suffering, I am called to give God glory.

If you're wondering how this all came to be, don't think for a second that I realized this from the beginning. Looking back, it's almost as if God would put a drop in a bucket every day until one day I was holding an entire bucket filled with blessings and hope and grace. I saw the treasure I was holding and excitedly dumped the bucket of grace over my head and felt it cleanse me from within.

What I gained from cancer was far more than I lost. What God produced was more than He pruned.

You see, God isn't just with you in the darkness of weakened health; He is the only one doing something when everyone has walked away, when there is no light, and when all you feel is an unpleasant cold breeze and pinpoints of pain. God is your light, your warmth, and the only One who can lead you out with care and love.

He walked with me. He will walk with you.

Even when I walk
  through the darkest valley,
I will not be afraid,
  for you are close beside me. (Ps. 23:4)

Humbled Through Cancer

In *All of Grace,* C. H. Spurgeon wrote, "The medicine is for the diseased; the quickening is for the dead; the pardon is for the guilty; liberation is for those who are bound; the opening of eyes is for those who are blind."[6]

More than I needed a physical surgeon to remove the cancer from my body, I needed God's healing medicine because of my diseased heart. Scripture calls that process sanctification.

Consider Jesus' words:

> "Healthy people don't need a doctor—sick people do." Then he added, "Now go and learn the meaning of this Scripture: 'I want you to show mercy, not offer sacrifices.' For I have come to call not those who think they are righteous, but those who know they are sinners." (Matt. 9:12–13)

Spiritually speaking, we're all sick. The prophet Jeremiah said it this way:

> "The human heart is the most deceitful of all things, and desperately wicked. Who really knows how bad it is? But I, the LORD, search all hearts and examine secret motives. I give all people their due rewards, according to what their actions deserve." (Jer. 17:9–10)

Our hearts are prone to sin, drawn toward evil, and wicked above all else. Cancer was my reminder that my heart is sick and that I need Christ hour by hour. Getting sick put my heart under a microscope and oh, how uncomfortable it was! It's humbling to see your need and your depravity. It's humbling to see your weakness and sinful tendencies. I need Christ to daily fill me with the Holy Spirit and to be a faithful doctor by getting rid of what isn't pleasing to Him and what is ultimately hurting me.

You and I, sinners alike, wicked in heart, are the whole reason the gospel is needed. Do we see it that way? Do we see our need for a Savior? I think before cancer I wasn't so concerned with such things. I knew I needed Christ, but by then having a cancer cut out of me made me recognize the spiritual lessons of a God who purifies through pain and humbles through hardships. Sanctification is spiritual surgery. Though the process is often painful, it is necessary to make us more like Christ and strong in Him.

The apostle Paul described it this way:

> Since you have heard about Jesus and have learned the truth that comes from him, throw off your old sinful nature and your former way of life, which is corrupted by lust and deception. Instead, let the Spirit renew your thoughts and attitudes. Put on your new nature, created to be like God—truly righteous and holy. (Eph. 4:21–24)

Daily Dependence

I met a woman at one of my speaking events a few years back who was walking through cancer. She was a young mom with little children. I understood how she felt when she expressed her anxieties, worries, plans, and doubts, and I understood how she could be sick yet still finding joy. Sadly, her cancer journey ended quickly, and she passed away a year later. It shook me up. I only met her that one time, but it was a reminder of how fleeting our lives are. The Lord determines our steps and our last breaths.

It was humbling and hard to hear the news of her going home to be with Jesus because walking through a health challenge can feel so helpless, as if we know nothing. Everything feels unknown, and the heightened emotions can drag us up high peaks and drop us into low valleys. But in the nothingness, we have something that is our everything, and that is a relationship with Jesus our Lord and Savior.

Our tragedy isn't forever because heaven is forever.

Healing is painful but our tragedy is temporary. Much as we've talked about in this book already, our tragedy isn't forever because *heaven* is forever. We can know that all suffering will have an end. Trials might not end in the way we'd hoped, like when a young mom dies from cancer, but they will surely end. If I've learned anything, it's that the healing of our souls is far more important than the healing of our bodies.

> Our bodies are buried in brokenness, but they will be raised in glory. They are buried in weakness, but they will be raised in strength. (1 Cor. 15:43)

God wants to make you well and find strength in Him. He wants you to be spiritually strong, and that happens through this process of sanctification. *Jesus died to make you whole.* Maybe that's through physical healing, but even more He wants to heal the ailments that no one sees and remove the hidden diseases that are keeping you from living in victory. That is what matters most.

Even as I write this today while "cancer free," I still have annual appointments, blood work, and scans. I'm dealing with a stress/heat rash from a life in the humid South and too many annoyances that I can't manage on my own. I still deal with precancerous moles on my body that have to be surgically excised, and I'm balancing medication and doing my best to keep myself healthy. These health challenges will always be a part of my experience in this life, but there will be an end in glory.

As my body wastes away on earth, my soul springs up and

blossoms in His strength. He gives me the strength to support my husband, to love my kids and to homeschool, to feed our farm animals and be a good steward of the land and home He's given us, to sing and dance while I make dinner for my family, to love my friends and church well and do my best as an author and speaker.

The trust in God that is birthed from our weakening health is a gift in and of itself. You have a choice to turn away from God and refuse to believe He has you. Or you can trust God with your kids, health, family, life, treatment, and your plans. The more challenges you go through, the more opportunity to let the Lord be your strength. Over time, you get to a place of total dependence because you recognize you have zero answers or solutions and you are helpless. But in our helplessness, we find true strength—His strength.

Putting on our new nature isn't a once and for all. It's a daily process that requires daily grace.

Let's recall Paul's words from Ephesians 4. When he reminds us to "put on our new nature" (v. 24), it's not a once and for all.

It's a daily process that requires daily grace.

Consider the Israelites as they wandered in the wilderness. They didn't receive manna all at once or enough for a week, but just enough for each day as their dependence on the Lord was being built. The same goes for us and our strength in Him. This becomes undeniable when we are sick or in physical pain. God doesn't just pour down His strength on us so we can do one month's worth of work and be superwoman in a day. It's a consistency of grace, ever flowing from the glory of heaven as He provides us with what we need for *today*.

That should bring us hope because we don't have to worry about tomorrow when our health is failing us and weakening our bodies. God will give you all that you need for today whether you're lying in a bed sick, living with chronic pain trying to find moments of reprieve to get you through, or recognizing your weaknesses as a stay-at-home mom who doesn't know how she will push past the exhaustion to get through until bedtime.

God doesn't give up on you. God doesn't walk away when you're talking or grab His phone as a distraction when you need Him the most. God is there and He is your answer when your strength is gone.

Practical Reminders

Ongoing health battles can feel debilitating, so let me share some practical statements to help us remember that something good is growing in the midst of the struggle.

This too shall pass

Sometimes the only helpful thing to say out loud is, *this too shall pass*. It's an audible reminder that this isn't the end.

God has me

God isn't checked out, forgetful, or careless. He has you. Could He heal you? Absolutely. But His ways are higher and we don't know what is best for us spiritually in the long term. Maybe you are bringing Him the most glory as you walk in weakness. Maybe God is using physical weakness to heal your deeper, spiritual needs.

Bodies fail, but my soul is strengthened

We will all wither away but our souls will remain strong in Him.

While reminders are helpful, the Word always remains our guide. We often talk about sharing in His sufferings, but it's a beautiful reminder in every one of these chapters to find honor and strength and privilege knowing you are suffering with and for Christ (Phil. 1:29).

In her book *Living Sacrifice*, Helen Roseveare says, "To love the Lord my God with all my strength will involve a physical cost. I must give Him my body to indwell, and through which to speak, whether He chooses by health or sickness, by strength or weakness, and trust Him utterly with the outcome."[7]

The problem we run into as a culture today is that we think we can't be strong if we are physically weak. And if we are weak, we become lumped in the "worthless" or "useless" category. But I beg to differ. Some of the mentally and spiritually strongest people I know have walked through the fire of their physical strength being ripped from them. What we see is another trial by fire through the very essence of our bodies being taken from us. The natural person thinks we have nothing left, when really God is just getting started with His transforming heart work.

When you are stripped of health, you finally see what matters. The things you believed were the glue that held your life together and what made you whole no longer matter. When you realize through your body weakening that the glue is not in your health or strength or the physicality that makes you, then you finally see that it is Christ who holds you together. While you're trying to hold yourself together by all the things we can see in the physical, God wants to piece you back and hold you together with His Son in the spiritual.

> So we don't look at the troubles we can see now; rather, we fix our gaze on things that cannot be seen. For the things we see now will soon be gone, but the things we cannot see will last forever. (2 Cor. 4:18)

That's why, whether you're stuck in bed or running a marathon, you have purpose and a calling and strength. Our lives are not marked by what we do, but by who we serve.

Is your only definition of a strong life one in which you are producing and creating and living in your own mustered-up strength? Strength in yourself is weakness. Weakness in Christ is strength.

Are you being sanctified through the understanding that even in the migraines and diagnosis and disease and pain you are still His?

He's not done, this is not the end of your story. You are in the chapters where God wants to do a good thing in you . . . today.

Loving the Lord your God with all of your strength will involve a physical cost because you give up your rights and allow Him to work in and through you in whatever way brings Him the most glory. This is a beautiful start to your sanctification as you become a woman of strength!

Weakness in His Strength

> All of this is for your benefit. And as God's grace reaches more and more people, there will be great thanksgiving, and God will receive more and more glory. That is why we never give up. Though our bodies are dying, our spirits are being renewed every day. For our present troubles are small and won't last very long. Yet they produce for us a glory that vastly outweighs them and will last forever! (2 Cor. 4:15–17)

When I was healing from cancer, if you had come up to me and quoted this passage and said, "Nicole, this is small and won't last very long," I probably would have told you to leave. It's just not what you want to hear in the midst of your suffering and health challenges. While you know in your heart of hearts that your situation won't be like this forever, the pain can be so consuming that you literally cannot see any hope or light ahead.

Physical trials can be some of the worst because there's no relief in the moment. You can't just write down what you're grateful for and feel better. You can't even get up and go for a walk because sometimes you're confined to your bed. There are no quick fixes to physical pain. And that truth makes it extremely challenging for those who want to blaze through life or indulge in instant gratification. While you know what you need, things like fresh air or a walk with a friend, you physically can't make those things happen. Your body fails in ways that nothing else can make up for, except Christ. There is no physical strength or magic pill, so in turn, God has to be our strength.

It's in those times where I need you to remember who and what is your strength. Yes, we know it's the Lord, but what does that actually mean?

> Three different times I begged the Lord to take [my suffering] away. Each time he said, "My grace is all you need. My power works best in weakness." So now I am glad to boast about my weaknesses, so that the power of Christ can work through me. That's why I take pleasure in my weaknesses, and in the insults, hardships, persecutions, and troubles that I suffer for Christ. For when I am weak, then I am strong. (2 Cor. 12:8–10)

The apostle Paul wrote this passage and he was very familiar with suffering himself. In fact, as he reminds us, "We have been beaten, been put in prison, faced angry mobs, worked to exhaustion, endured sleepless nights, and gone without food" (2 Cor. 6:5). And that's just the beginning of what he faced.

But what I love about 2 Corinthians 12 is that Paul says he would rather boast and pride himself in his sufferings and weaknesses because he knows that Christ would get the glory out of his life all the more. When we're weak, we can't stand on anything to make us look better or heal us faster. We are where we are in our weakness and there is no changing that. Christ is exalted in seasons like that because He's the only strength for each day that we

Ask Him to do the heart work that sanctifies you into His likeness so that at the end of your life when your body is failing you, you can gaze in His eyes for the first time, humbled, and knowing it was all worth it for the sake of boasting in Him.

have. Christ dwells where He is invited, and from personal experience, when I am weak, I ask for more of Him. When I am strong, I can easily forget my need.

Weakness reveals our need for a Savior. Your sickness or diagnosis or disease or ailment or health challenges are humbling you, and God is doing a sanctifying work through you because of this season. There is nothing better than having times in our lives where we know without a doubt how much we need Him. As great as this is, I also understand how difficult it is to live out.

Try today, instead of praying that God heals your body, praying that He continues to heal your soul. Ask Him to do the heart work that sanctifies you into His likeness so that at the end of your life when your body is failing you, you can gaze in His eyes for the first time, humbled, and knowing it was all worth it for the sake of boasting in Him. For when you were weak, He was so strong, and that not only brought Him glory, but others saw that nothing stops God from working in and through His people.

I know you catch yourself saying similar things as I have like, "What is the point of this?" But can I tell you that every day, every long, drawn-out, physically painful day, God is adding another drop to your bucket. And when you get to meet Him face-to-face, that bucket of grace will wash over you and purify you and cleanse you from within so that you can stand rightly before Christ and say, it was all worth it for the sake of knowing You, Jesus.

Blooming in the Dark

Something Good to Remember: The more our health weakens, the more opportunity for Christ to be our strength.

For Reflection: How can you depend on Him more in your weakness this week?

For Meditation: 2 Corinthians 12:9

To Pray: *Lord I am struggling! I recognize my need for You. Thank You that You are my strength in all of my weaknesses and in every challenging season of my life. Thank You that regardless of how I feel, I know You are doing an inner work in me. I ask that You heal my body, but I'd rather You continue Your sanctifying work by healing my soul. Give me Your strength for today. I love You, Lord.*

chapter 9

When You're Tired of Trying: Obedience in Christ

So let's not get tired of doing what is good. At just the right time we will reap a harvest of blessing if we don't give up.

GALATIANS 6:9

Something Good Will Grow

The fruit of obedience is intimacy with Jesus. This is the only pathway to true contentment.

It's so easy to continuously pour into our families, friends, job, prayer, and people, yet not see fruit in the way we want to or as quickly as we want. Here's the rub: Biblically speaking, fruit is always the evidence of sowing. When you're surrendered to Christ, there *will* be fruit.

John 15:4–5 records Jesus' words:

> "Remain in me, and I will remain in you. For a branch cannot produce fruit if it is severed from the vine, and you cannot be fruitful unless you remain in me. Yes, I am the vine; you are the branches. Those who remain in me, and I in them, will produce much fruit. For apart from me you can do nothing."

If you're connected to the vine, Jesus, He will bear fruit in your life. Sometimes it's just hard to accept that our fruit might be an apple when we wanted it to be an orange. We are Christ's and God is our Creator, which means He gets to decide what fruit comes from our lives.

Seeing the Unseen

Seeing the fruit isn't always the issue. What's difficult is the lack of reward and the exhaustion from never-ending trying. Sometimes I am just flat-out tired of trying. You too?

We know we won't always see our rewards or the blessings of longsuffering this side of eternity, but where can we turn when we're exhausted from doing the right thing, over and over again? What happens when you are tired of trying and honestly just tired of obedience? What about when it all feels . . . pointless? What happens when you don't have it in you to keep going and the grind of life is beating you down?

That's when we need to be obedient to Christ all the more.

I know full well that the word "obedient" is sometimes cringeworthy because it's up there with the "submission" and "discipline"—words that our flesh doesn't like. But my goal in this chapter is to prove to you that a life of submission to Christ, an obedient life, is the most joy-filled and beautiful life.

To be honest, this chapter wasn't fun to write. It might not be fun to read either. Our flesh, meaning our sin nature, is strong and we cave easily into our exhaustion or entitlement as if God owes us something from our hard work.

Let's fight our sin nature together. As we do, we'll learn to find fulfillment in the steadfast love and character of Christ. Let this chapter speak to you if you find yourself in a season where your obedience doesn't seem to be getting you anywhere. When everyone around you is "working hard" and getting high fives and worldly blessings—and you find yourself carrying a load far heavier with no results of your strength and faith—believe that something good is growing. Often, that something good is a deeper intimacy with our Savior.

We need to get to a place where our obedience to Christ, regardless of the daily grind, is what supersedes the desire to be rewarded or appreciated. We choose to obey because we love our Savior. And in that sweet spot of choosing our Savior again and again, we have a contentment and joy that will last a lifetime.

Our goal is to get to a place where we are joyfully obeying and out of that comes contentment in Christ, even when life is exhausting.

I understand how hard this is. I'm a stay-at-home, homeschooling, farm mom, and many of my efforts go unnoticed. But the unseen places of my life are where I've learned that there is great joy in obedience to Christ. Our goal is to get to a place where we are joyfully obeying and out of that comes contentment in Christ, even when life is exhausting.

Contentment Follows Obedience

There is always work on our farm, The Faithful Homestead. With kids and animals and land and old fences, an older country farmhouse, a pond, and a creek, we constantly have work to do. We have things to fix, acreage to clean up, fences to mend, animals to care for, and projects to start. You've heard the phrase "never a dull moment"—it's true! I bet the same is true in your home.

One of our homestead rules is "Never say you're bored around Mom." I will give you a project within seconds because the work is never finished. And as a black-and-white thinker, the concept that our farm will never be complete is hard for me to grasp. I often find myself thinking, *I'll be so happy when this project is finished.*

Instead of being thankful *now*, happy *now*, content *now*, I've noticed how I'm usually on to the next thing. Unfortunately, when I do that, I forget the best parts of life when I obey. My fellowship with God and others remains unbroken when I obey His command to forgive. My body works better when I obey God's command to rest. When I reject self-sufficiency and lean on Jesus, as He's asked me to, my anxiety goes way down. Obedience really is the pathway to true contentment. I don't want to forget to take a deep breath and see all that God has given me. That's what matters: a faithful, obedient, content life in Christ.

> If we're not consistently showing up, little by little every day with the Lord, when the big trials come, we'll be left with no spiritual resources to get us through.

What I have noticed over time is that if I don't work a little every day, our "days off" are way too busy, which then produces a feeling of being overwhelmed.

The same concept applies in our walk with the Lord when we're exhausted from the daily tasks, burdens, and hurts of life. If we're not consistently showing up, little by little every day with the Lord (and for the people around us), when the big trials of life come, we'll be left with no spiritual resources, knowledge, or strength to get us through.

This is all a part of our obedience in Christ. Does it take discipline to wake up early to spend time with the Lord? Yes. But it's always worth it. Is it sometimes thankless going to the same job, dealing with the same people, feeling unappreciated, and then waking up and doing it all over again the next day? Yes. Is it exhausting to work so hard all day, only to realize you barely have enough to pay your bills? Yes. But in that obedience to love the Lord and serve your family, or provide for yourself, you are learning that it's not about what you do and how hard you work; it's about honoring Jesus with every part of your life.

The more we obey, the more content we'll be, wanting for nothing but Christ. Even Jesus understood that not all obedience looks rewarding in the world's eyes. But through God's eyes, Jesus' obedience brought salvation to the world. "He humbled himself in obedience to God and died a criminal's death on a cross" (Phil. 2:8).

Our obedience will be rewarded by the Lord, but it won't always be understood by the world. Very few looked at Jesus' death on the cross as fruitful or as a reward for His obedience. Little did they know at the time, Jesus' obedient act would change the course of history.

Maybe your obedience doesn't bring about high fives and gold stars, but God sees. You're storing up treasures in heaven.

We're most discontent when we are not aligned with Christ, but contentment in Him is the fulfillment of a rhythm of obedience. Since it is obedience that keeps us close to Jesus, and disobedience separates us from Him, can we truly be content when we are living in rebellion? While disobedience breeds pain and a discontent heart, obedience brings life, joy, and contentment.

For example, whenever I am unforgiving, short-tempered, or not in the Word, I am most discontent. But when I am forgiving, honest, and in step with the Spirit, I will reap the rewards of doing the right thing. Same for you. Maybe you won't get noticed or appreciated. Maybe your obedience doesn't bring about high fives and gold stars, but God sees. He sees and it's all a part of storing up treasures in heaven.

> "Store your treasures in heaven, where moths and rust cannot destroy, and thieves do not break in and steal. Wherever your treasure is, there the desires of your heart will also be."
> (Matt. 6:20–21)

When you are abiding in Christ your life may not be easy, but the day-to-day simplicity of being guided by our Creator should ease you into a sacred place of contentment where your heart is truly satisfied.

A Harvest of Blessing

At the moment, I am tired of trying in so many ways. While trying itself is not a bad thing, it's when the trying starts to take away your peace, joy, or rest that it can get messy. We get into trouble when our trying to be excellent becomes proving and striving and carrying burdens that aren't meant for us.

Have you been there? The problem isn't competition with anyone else but yourself. It's a mind game that we have to constantly surrender to the Lord or else we get caught up in a works-based religion instead of a grace-filled relationship and faith in Christ. "How foolish can you be?" Paul asks in Galatians 3:3. "After starting your new lives in the Spirit, why are you now trying to become perfect by your own human effort?"

God sees your heart motives and desire to serve Him. That's a beautiful obedience.

We can't do it on our own. No amount of trying in our own effort will get us anywhere. I even caught myself not opening the Word or praying before I started writing this chapter! A few minutes in and I realized I have nothing beneficial to offer you on my own and need the Lord's guidance and peace before ever starting my day or tasks. It's foolish to try to earn approval or rewards. Foolish also means unwise, thoughtless, or irrational. The words "foolish" or "fools" are in the Bible over a hundred times, usually talking about wisdom and folly and guiding us to understand the consequences of rejecting the Lord's ways. In other words, being disobedient. Being unwise. Being a fool. I sure don't want to be like that! When we understand that we have nothing to prove, and that God is already for us if we are His, then we don't get tired of trying. Instead, we have the joy of obeying.

> So let's not get tired of doing what is good. At just the right time we will reap a harvest of blessing if we don't give up. (Gal. 6:9)

This blessing of obedience is sanctification, the process of becoming more like Jesus. Obedience also keeps us in unbroken fellowship with Him. Sin and rebellion separate. Obedience unites. When you reject the idea that you have something to prove, your striving turns to surrender and you finally lift your eyes and rest in God's plan for your life. You might want to show the world what you have to offer, but that will only get you so far in your own strength.

Success in the world's eyes is far different than success in the Christian's life. God sees your heart motives and desire to serve Him, no matter the cost. That's a beautiful obedience.

The Seed of Obedience

In Matthew 13:1–23, Jesus tells a parable of a farmer planting seeds. It's about how the kind of soil you plant in matters. Read through the story and Jesus' explanation; I'll give you a few minutes.

Which soil best describes you?

Let's talk about the seed that fell on the rocky soil. This represents those who hear the message and immediately receive it with joy. But since they don't have deep roots, they don't last long. They fall away as soon as they have problems or are persecuted for believing God's Word.

How do you get deep roots? It's with little-by-little, step-by-step obedience.

I'm sure it wasn't easy for Mary to carry the Son of God or for Noah to build an ark. I'm sure Moses wasn't comfortable speaking and leading a nation to the promised land. I'm sure Peter and James and John and the other disciples weren't always comfortable obeying and learning from Jesus as He flipped the culture on its head.

Obeying the Lord isn't always an easy task because it is the opposite of what your sinful nature—the flesh—wants to do. Just this week, out of obedience to the Lord, I found these ordinary opportunities to be obedient:

- Called someone to apologize for my lack of communication and letting my anger get the best of me
- Said yes to a project I preferred to say no to
- Bought a new homeschool curriculum that would be better for my kids but more work for me
- Invited a family over even though I was exhausted
- Met with our church's care pastor to work through some difficult situations

What's on your list of recent step-by-step opportunities for obedience?

I would have rather not done any of those things. Honestly! Obeying God isn't always fun and it is rarely rewarded in the ways you think are best for you. But from my week above, what came from my obedience? Wisdom, understanding, reliance on the Lord, community . . . these are the things we should be celebrating!

I want to surround myself with people who celebrate a Christian sister's surrender because they know that obedience to Christ will sanctify us all the more. You're more like Jesus today? Cheers to that!

Start looking at how God is growing you through your obedience.

A Heart of Obedience

I have been in situations where God asked me to do something and I fought Him on it. I made excuses, I tried to redirect my life into another lane, I asked questions, I doubted whether I was really hearing clearly from the Lord. Ultimately, I lacked obedience.

As a mother of four, if I ask my kids to do something, I hope they listen and obey the first time. God doesn't get angry as I would if I had to keep asking them to listen or obey, but do we ever think about how our sin and disobedience hurts the heart of the Father?

When we are sinned against, when our kids don't obey advice that's coming from a place of love, when we're rejected . . . that all hurts and grieves our hearts. If every sin is ultimately against God, how much more does He hurt when we sin, disobey, and reject Him?

Your disobedience reveals a painful reality: We obey who we trust.

I'm sure you know by now that I believe everything starts with a foundation in Christ and knowing God's character and His heart. Out of that, everything flows and starts to make sense.

Part of obedience is laying down expectations of what you think is best. This is what *I* want to learn. This is what *I* want to have happen. This is the job *I* want. This is the outcome *I* want. This is how *I* want things to go.

> When we don't see the fruit or outcomes we want from years of trying, we have to go back to the basics. Jesus first.

Notice a theme? Those questions are the driving force to why we even started trying in the first place. The relationships and money and growth and opportunities become bigger than the main thing: a relationship with Jesus. We have elevated the outcome and the prize and the fruit of trying above Jesus. We care more about what we get out of obedience instead of focusing on the firm foundation we're establishing with Christ.

We're chasing after the wind.

This is why when we don't see the fruit or outcomes we want from years of prayer and building and developing and helping and serving, we have to go back to the basics. Jesus first. Obedience and submission to Christ.

> Of course, you get no credit for being patient if you are beaten for doing wrong. But if you suffer for doing good and endure it patiently, God is pleased with you. For God called you to do good, even if it means suffering, just as Christ suffered for you. He is your example, and you must follow in his steps.
> (1 Peter 2:20–21)

The Blessings in Obedience

When I look at the people in the Bible, I see a common thread. A lot of tribulations and pain came to their lives and even to the lives of others from their lack of obedience. Here are a few; likely you can think of more.

- Adam and Eve disobeyed God and ate the fruit, which resulted in the fall of humankind.
- Lot's wife disobeyed God and turned back to look at the destruction of Sodom and Gomorrah, and was turned to a pillar of salt.
- The Israelites disobeyed by turning to idols, complaining, and not trusting God's ways, so their entry into the promised land was delayed by forty years.
- Jonah disobeyed God by going in the opposite direction of where the Lord was sending him. He ended up in the belly of a great fish for three days and finally went to Nineveh anyway.
- Samson disobeyed God by revealing the secret to his strength, resulting in a loss of that strength and a gruesome end.

The list could go on. When I look at these examples, I am reminded that our obedience to the Lord is in direct correlation to suffering well and God growing something good in our lives.

In fact, Galatians 5:24 talks about how those who belong to Christ have nailed their passions and desires of their sinful nature to His cross and crucified them there! Out of obedience, as a genuine believer, have you nailed your sin to the cross?

The deeper heart work here is that if we are claiming to love Christ, and we want to grow in Him, that means we take on the truth that our life is not our own anymore. Our flesh hates that, but we grow in character, endurance, hope, and obedience the more we step toward Christ and turn from sin.

I know our faith is not works-based and I know obedience is work (at first anyway), but ultimately if we are in relationship with God, trusting Him through our pain, and practicing daily obedience, our suffering will be turned to something beautiful *in time*.

If we are in relationship with God, trusting Him through our pain, and practicing daily obedience, our suffering will be turned to something beautiful in time.

So how do we do that? How do we obey God? Well, that could be an entire book on its own, but for you and for me, it can look like this in our daily life: submit to Him.

Surrendering to Christ brings freedom. Freedom means you are not the one who has to have it all together, know it all, plan it all, heal in your timing, or control. It's a relief to submit to the One who knows all and loves us deeply.

To put it into perspective, think of it this way. Have you ever been on a date or even out with one of your best friends after you're exhausted from the day? Maybe you had a hard day at work or you're overstimulated from being at home with the kids all day. Isn't it so nice to have someone plan an outing, pick you up, and maybe even treat you, while you just get to enjoy the evening? That's how I like to think of submission when it comes to trusting the Lord. Letting Him lead. Letting Him guide. Letting Him reveal what's best. In the end, it's *so* freeing and helpful as it takes the pressure off ourselves to have it all together. Aren't you tired of trying? Obeying Him through submission will bring good things to your life.

Listen to Him

Reading the Word and giving Him the space to speak to us is an act of obedience. Maybe that means you go on a walk every day and you don't fill the time by listening to a podcast or calling a friend but instead you quiet yourself and be sensitive to what the Spirit brings to mind. Or maybe you squeeze in reading the Word at some point during the day instead of just morning or night and you take the time to reflect on what you read. Is God saying something through your spouse, a friend, or a pastor? Opening our spiritual ears to God helps put Him first.

Serve Others

Serving and loving others is an act of obedience that may be both immediately rewarding and challenging in the long-term. Intentionally serving other people in love is an obvious, hands-on way to be obedient.

We may serve through an organized effort such as a church, community organization, or a larger project; or we may do so quietly when only the person we're serving knows about our effort. Our flesh might be tempted to want recognition or at least acknowledgment. We want our service to be validated. But it isn't always. You might shop for an older neighbor and she's critical you purchased the wrong brand of plastic wrap instead of thanking you for taking time out of your day. You pour yourself out on the food drive your church runs and your name was left off the list in the bulletin thanking the volunteers. When things like this happen repeatedly, you might be tempted to give up.

Don't. Your contentment depends on your obedience, not on others' affirmation. It's not about the fruit being produced or the rewards that are happening, it's about our obedience to Christ and how that will produce more fruit than we ever could have prayed for.

Press into Him. Go against the grain and obey at all costs. Even if it doesn't make sense, even if it's uncomfortable or exhausting, even if you see no purpose or fruit, obey and press in. Believe the best. Trust. Keep going. And do it again tomorrow.

Blooming in the Dark

Something Good to Remember: When you're exhausted from striving, take a small step of obedience.

For Reflection: Do you obey God for the sake of a reward? Or does your love and relationship with God draw you to obedience?

For Meditation: 1 Peter 2:21

To Pray: *Lord, I am so tired of doing everything on my own. Help me obey You, serve You, and focus on what You have for me, even in the midst of my exhaustion from striving. I believe You are the reward, and a relationship with You is the greatest prize. Thank You for patiently guiding me when I need it the most. Amen.*

chapter 10

When Depression Takes Root: Purpose in Christ

You are a chosen people. You are royal priests, a holy nation, God's very own possession. As a result, you can show others the goodness of God, for he called you out of the darkness into his wonderful light.

1 PETER 2:9

Something Good Will Grow

God uses the darkness of depression to help us see the light of Christ and our purpose in Him.

Winter seems to be many people's least favorite time of year. Christmas season is always the best and filled with hope, and then there tends to be a long, uninvited lull leading into spring. Sometimes the needed rainstorms, random fluffy snow, or sprinkled in sunshine can make the months a tad more bearable. But for many, the cold, muddy seasons are difficult and dreaded.

Blinded from All Things Good

What I have found is that seasonal depression can rear its ugly head while the ground is wet and colorless, the trees are lifeless, the sky is overcast and dark, and the flower beds are bare. I can sense myself craving a tropical beach or fresh blooms growing in the garden. While I'm naturally a creative and joyful person, the winter strips me of inspiration as my soul feels as if it wilted with the plants. I know I'm not alone; perhaps you also experience blues from the drabness of winter.

I've also experienced severe depression (sometimes described as clinical depression) in multiple seasons of my life, which are much more serious than the blues. I had postpartum depression after two of my babies, depression after my miscarriage, depression during the season following my sexual assault, and for a short time after cancer. Essentially, when I'm faced with life-altering trials and trauma, I know that feelings of purposelessness and depression are not far off.

For those who experience depression, almost nothing else causes such severe hopelessness. For me, it's almost as if I have an unseen trigger in the deepest part of my soul that is flipped and my eyes are completely blinded from all things good and beautiful. Maybe you've experienced this too.

The scary part is that nothing can pull me out when I'm depressed. It's as though I'm being pressured by a friend to go on the worst ride at the county fair. I never want to go on it, I want to get off before I even get on, I feel nauseated and I complain the entire time.

Depression is that terrible carnival ride, but worse. The hopelessness that comes with depression can feel unbearable. It's the worst I've ever felt and the most negative and purposeless place I've ever been. I hope you haven't experienced this, but unfortunately, depression is so prevalent that it's important for us to talk about it.

While we won't be tackling the clinical side of depression (because this is more severe and beyond the scope of this book), we will be talking about the spiritual side of depression and the persistent feeling of sadness and hopelessness it brings: those heavy and dark times we face—when we lose all enjoyment in daily life and we feel like we're walking through a dark cloud—that have us craving light again.

If you are walking through depression right now, what I most want you to hear is that there is hope. Not in a "Do these five things to make yourself feel better" way. Those who have experienced depression know there is no to-do list that will eliminate the feeling. Rather, let's reframe depression and talk about the hope and purpose in it. Because, believe it or not, there is purpose.

When we talk about depression, it has to be through a lens of truth and what we already know about God.

This chapter is for every woman. Many of us have all been in the place of sadness or gloom where we can't seem to climb out of our dark trench.

But *the* most important thing to consider before going on is our fundamental core beliefs about God. In chapter 2 we talked about how insecurity can paralyze us but that we are also victorious in Christ because we are His—chosen, His masterpiece, called and adopted into His family. In chapter 4 we talked about people failing us, yet God never will because He is always tenderhearted, loving and drawing us closer. In chapter 6 we talked about God being faithful and the only trustworthy one.

The reason I'm bringing these chapters up again is because when we talk about depression, it has to be through a lens of *truth* and what we *already know* about God. The truth that God is good and faithful, merciful and kind. Consider these five questions:

1. Is God good?
2. Does He love you?
3. Is He always faithful?
4. Is He sovereign?
5. Can you trust Him?

God *Is* Good

We must know who God is and know who He says we are, or else our seasons of darkness and depression will be that much harder. If you need to take thirty minutes to go back and read chapter 2 and meditate on Ephesians 1, go ahead and do so. We have to be in a truth-filled frame of mind before going forward.

After I was raped, you can imagine how low and depressed I was. There was nothing that could get me out of my dark, lifeless, and hopeless hole. I pretended I was fine over time but at the core of me, I was wrecked and broken and would have been perfectly fine if Jesus took me home so I wouldn't have to deal with living this nightmare.

When you walk through horrible things that turn everything you once believed upside down, you don't look in the mirror and smile or even recognize the dead eyes staring back at you. There are no magic words or answers that help. I felt like I was drowning in purposelessness during that dark season.

Looking back, how did God do it? How did He pull me through? Little by little, a slow trek in unfamiliar territory. It was putting one foot in front of the next and receiving whatever I could from God and others on a daily basis. Prayers, community, a hug, a listening ear, a warm meal, a word of encouragement, a song, space, a good night's rest, kindness . . . the list goes on. I wish I could give you five steps toward healing after trauma so that you don't ever have to face depression, but I'd be doing God a disservice because He's the only One who has beautifully mapped your road back to hope.

"When they walk through the Valley of Weeping, it will become a place of refreshing springs. The autumn rains will clothe it with blessings" (Ps. 84:6). When I read this verse, it reminds me that my weeping will turn to a wellspring of hope because I serve a faithful God. We all walk through difficult journeys of sorrow and life's trials, but God will transform your weeping too in this season of depression into wellsprings of hope. There is blessing and refreshment in the midst of depression available to those who are His. "Those who plant in tears will harvest with shouts of joy" (Ps. 126:5).

God is a personal God and He knows what's best for you going forward. But if I can share anything about depression after loss or trauma, it's to keep going with open hands. It's saying honestly to God, "I don't know how I'll ever get out of this dark place, but I trust that You are here with me and will guide me out." Healing is not linear, but maybe today you get out of bed. And tomorrow you brush your teeth. And the next day you eat a bowl of cereal. And the next day you shower.

Healing is not linear, but maybe today you get out of bed. And tomorrow you brush your teeth.

It was always the small and slow steps that God used to gently guide me out of my depression. Each step had purpose.

God Is for You

After a rough first year in college, I went on a mission trip to India. While I was there, I got to teach the Bible from a makeshift wooden pulpit in a small cement-walled hall that was the church. The title of my message was "God Is for Us." I quoted Psalm 118 and said, "The Lord answered me and set me free! He is for you and has set you free!" While I felt odd at first speaking through a translator, trying to focus on when to pause and what to emphasize, I knew that I was just the messenger, and the Lord is always gracious to use our "trying." Speaking the Word after a hard year gave me purpose.

But who knew that only a year after the mission trip to India, I would face the most traumatic event and be raped by a stranger. I desperately needed those words, "God Is for Me," for myself.

While it didn't *feel* like God was for me because of the circumstances He allowed, God was still for me. He didn't cause the rape.

Being raped was a horrific act of injustice against His daughter. From it, I've learned:

- This world is filled with evil and heartache, and the devil and his demons will do whatever it takes to steal our identity, kill our faith, and destroy what little hope we had left.
- Jesus bore every awful and appalling sin on the cross two thousand years ago.
- God was angry when that happened to me and we can stand on His justice, knowing anyone who does wrong will be repaid for their wrongs (Col. 3:25).

While God maybe didn't stop evil from happening in your life, or didn't fully heal you when you were desperate, or answer when you wanted a response, you have to put your pain in its rightful place. There is evil and there is good. And God is always on the side of good.

By God's grace, slowly—and I mean *very* slowly—God will continue to draw you to Himself when you know He's not the One to blame. When we remember and truly believe that He is for us and is in the business of redemption and restoration, we can get up another day.

When we remember and truly believe that He is for us and is in the business of redemption and restoration, we can get up another day.

Trauma and pain causes us to be blinded to reality. But know that you are not alone in this suffering through depression because not only do we all go through difficult times, there are many examples of people in the Bible who have gone through deep despair just like you. Let's relate to the example of Job and glean some helpful insight into what he did, and what God said as Job moved forward. Let's take a look at depression through a theological lens.

The Life of Job

I spoke at a pretty snazzy women's conference in a good part of town a while back, and yet I heard many women's stories in that church who had walked through similar or worse things than I have. We don't need to compare suffering, but it showed me that no matter where I go and who I talk to, pain and heartache is universal. We all have a testimony and we have all walked through pain and loss. Suffering does not discriminate.

But reading Job gives us another level of heartache, an unimaginable one. Even though Job lost his children, livestock, and everything he ever held on to or worked for, he did not doubt or blame the Lord. "In all this, Job did not sin by charging God with wrongdoing" (Job 1:22 NIV), but he boldly lamented to God, as we'll see.

Job then faced health issues as boils came over his entire body (Job 2:7). When his wife—and let's remember Job's wife was also suffering the loss of her children—suggested Job just "curse God and die" (Job 2:9), Job still exemplified righteousness and responded, "Should we accept only good things from the hand of God and never anything bad?"

Let's ask ourselves that same question. Should we only accept the good things from the Lord (e.g., health, family, babies, homes, food to eat, a bed to sleep in, a job, friends) but get upset with anything that disrupts our utopia? Who was I to think I could slide through life unaffected by the torments and evils of the world? We are not above the Suffering Servant, Jesus Himself, who chose suffering to save you and me.

Job seems as if he is maintaining strength in the Lord despite devastation. But then he gets to talking with his friends, listening to their opinions, trying to make sense of his circumstances, and really gets honest with the Lord.

- "You formed me with your hands; you made me, yet now you completely destroy me." (10:8)

- "My eyes are swollen with weeping, and I am but a shadow of my former self." (17:7)
- "The groans of the dying rise from the city, and the wounded cry for help, yet God ignores their moaning." (24:12)
- "And now my life seeps away. Depression haunts my days. At night my bones are filled with pain, which gnaws at me relentlessly. With a strong hand, God grabs my shirt. He grips me by the collar of my coat. He has thrown me into the mud. I'm nothing more than dust and ashes." (30:16–19)

Have you been there? Can you relate? As you read these verses, do you feel Job's words resonate with similar thoughts you've been having?

Job was filled with shame and misery, questions and anger. We get a glimpse into his conversations with God, his concerns, and his thoughts. We read his friends' opinions (which were mostly unhelpful), but then Job starts to get to a dark place.

Job sees his life and what was. He used to be wealthy, prosperous, respected, and hopeful. He used to be listened to and was a counsel to others. Job used to be valued. And now he is mocked and despised. He is opposed. "My honor has blown away in the wind, and my prosperity has vanished like a cloud. And now my life seeps away. Depression haunts my days. At night my bones are filled with pain" (30:15–17).

Then Job makes a lot of bold accusations against God in chapter 30:

"I cry to you . . . but you don't answer." (v. 20)

"I stand before you, but you don't even look." (v. 20)

"You have become cruel toward me." (v. 21)

"You use your power to persecute me." (v. 21)

"You throw me into the whirlwind and destroy me in the storm." (v. 22)

Job goes inward and examines himself. Had he turned away from the needy (30:24–25)? Had he lusted over a young woman (31:1)? Had he lied or deceived (31:5)? No, he was not guilty of these. He questions his heart, trying to make sense of his miserable life so he can put the blame on someone or something and find out the reason for his torments. What Job doesn't know is that all of this was due to the evil one offstage who bet God that Job wouldn't be faithful if his blessings were taken away.

The gracious smackdown happens in Job 38:

> Then the Lord answered Job from the whirlwind:
>
> "Who is this that questions my wisdom
> with such ignorant words?
> Brace yourself like a man,
> because I have some questions for you,
> and you must answer them. (vv. 1–3)
>
> Where were you when I laid the foundations of the earth?
> Tell me, if you know so much.
> Who determined its dimensions
> and stretched out the surveying line? (vv. 4–5)
> What supports its foundations,
> and who laid its cornerstone? (v. 6)
>
> Who kept the sea inside its boundaries? (v. 8)
>
> Have you ever commanded the morning to appear
> and caused the dawn to rise in the east? (v. 12)
>
> Have you made daylight spread to the ends of the earth? (v. 13)
>
> Have you explored the springs from which the seas come? (v. 16)
>
> Do you know where the gates of death are located? (v. 17)

Do you realize the extent of the earth?
Tell me about it if you know!" (v. 18)

God goes on and then adds, "But of course you know all this! For you were born before it was all created, and you are so very experienced!" (v. 21)

Take a few minutes to read chapters 38 and 39, because they're really quite convicting. These chapters are composed of questions from God to Job concerning the intricacies of life and creation and how things work that we'll never understand. Only God does because He is God . . . and we are not.

After the Lord's lengthy rebuke, Job says (42:2–5):

"I know that you can do anything,
and no one can stop you.
You asked, 'Who is this that questions my wisdom with such ignorance?'
It is I—and I was talking about things I knew nothing about,
things far too wonderful for me.
You said, 'Listen and I will speak!
I have some questions for you,
and you must answer them.'
I had only heard about you before,
but now I have seen you with my own eyes."

He then winds up in verse 6: "I take back everything I said, and I sit in dust and ashes to show my repentance" (42:6). While the book of Job is one of the most challenging to fully understand, we can follow Job's example by trusting and worshiping God even in the most brutal of situations. Job still had purpose—for one thing, he prayed for his friends who had given him misplaced advice and God accepted his prayer (42:8–10)—and he still had dignity because of his love for the Lord, not because of what he lacked.

You still have purpose and dignity, even in your deepest sorrow and darkest moment of despair. "Though he slay me, I will hope in him" (13:15a ESV).

A Tender Reminder

So often we have completely forgotten to have a holy fear of God in our depression. I say "we" because I am the first to be guilty of this.

As I studied Job for this chapter, I was reminded that I am nothing, purposeless, and lifeless apart from God. But with Him, I have *everything*. Purpose, life to the full, hope, dignity, confidence, strength, and beauty! It's so important in the middle of depression to focus on what God *has* done instead of what we're lacking. Focusing on who He is, instead of who we aren't.

I think our culture is so obsessed with people validating our feelings that we have forgotten the authority of God in the midst of what we're walking. Validating people's feelings has become more important than walking in truth, and when I do the same, my depression is always worse. We don't just have a "feeling of down in the dumps" problem. We have trust issues and a lack of understanding of who God is and what He says about us.

Job grieved. He spoke his mind. He wept. He called out to the Lord. He spoke honestly. He prayed. He questioned God. He lamented. He listened to friends' opinions.

But then Job got a long rebuke from the Lord and ended in humility and reverence toward almighty God.

We must do the same. Go there with God. Go to the dark places, ask the hard questions, admit the lingering doubts, and seek the counsel of godly friends. Go there with Him.

But then end in humility and reverence toward our holy and almighty God.

If you're depressed, I get it. More than you know. You are not in sin if you are depressed right now. Maybe make an appointment with your doctor; a change of diet or medication could be what's best for you in persistent, serious depression. But when it comes to sadness, feelings of being overwhelmed, and disappointments in life that cause extreme purposelessness and sorrow, consider the life of Job and remember who you serve.

Depression tells you that you don't matter. God tells you that you have purpose.

A. W. Tozer said it like this: "It might comfort one who finds himself in the middle of an emotional desert to know that his experience is not unique. The sweetest and holiest saints whose feet have graced this earth have at some time found themselves there."[8]

Depression can feel like a very "self-focused" problem. You're trusting in your abilities and strength to fix, heal, plan, and restore, when that should all be cast upon the cross where Jesus already proclaimed, "It is finished."

Depression tells you that you don't matter. God tells you that you have purpose.

Depression tells you that you're in charge of your messed-up life. God tells you He has authored your days and has a beautiful plan.

Depression tells you you're alone in your darkness. God tells you Jesus is walking with you and the Spirit is interceding for you.

Depression tells you it will always be this way. God says His mercies are new every morning.

Depression tells you your life is one big, unending disappointment. God says you are a new creation, called for good purposes, His masterpiece, and an heir to Christ.

While depression will run its inevitable course in seasons of your life, this is not where your story ends. I promise you that. If you can just keep holding on to Him for one more day, He will show up and meet you on the floor of your tears when evil surrounds and when no one else is coming to save you. He is the God who sees your pain, and already took your pain to the cross at Calvary, and now wants to transform your sorrows to purpose and joy in Christ.

He is close to the brokenhearted. He gives us strength for today and hope for tomorrow. Day by day.

Victory Is Sweeter After the Struggle

I've heard it said that you should check on your strongest and happiest friends, because it's often those types who have the darkest depression. I understand this. Consider Job's friends for a moment. Before they shared their opinions, they sat with Job for seven days and seven nights and didn't speak a word to him (Job 2:13). They knew his suffering was great and gave him the space to process and vent. We should do the same. When your friend who's in depression is expressing how they are doing, be quick to listen and to sit with them before jumping in with your "two cents." Then ask the Lord how to best respond in wisdom, love, and truth.

What I have noticed though, is that if we have never experienced the lows of depression, would we understand the mountaintop of joy and happiness?

Victory isn't as sweet if you've never experienced defeat. The prize or reward loses its luster if you didn't have to struggle and fight to earn it. Sometimes the women who struggle with depression have also experienced the sweetest joy of the Lord because they understand the burden of sorrows and emotional torment.

The only "right way" to heal is on your knees in surrender. We can't fix ourselves or trust only ourselves, or cause everything to work together in our own lives. Only God can.

Here are some weekly questions we can ask ourselves to stay centered emotionally:

What can I control and what can I release?

What am I stressed about that hasn't happened or that isn't happening right now?

Why am I worried about something out of my control?

Proverbs 12:25 (NKJV): "Anxiety in the heart of man causes depression, but a good word makes it glad."[9]

What is a good word? Truth. Not trite phrases, like "You got this! You'll be fine! Pull yourself out! Let it go! Snap out of it!"

In all things, go to the Father. He has called you out of darkness, and now it's time to step into the light full of purpose. You were created for a reason, and your pain is not wasted.

But instead, truth. Our sovereign and kind Lord—Creator of heaven and earth, faithful in all, our provider, King of kings waiting for His bride, orchestrator of all things holy and good, love that never ends, sacrificial—has a plan and purpose for *you*. He created you on purpose with purpose to glorify Him and, in that process of glorifying Him, you will bloom and grow.

It's okay to not be okay. It's okay to hurt and heal and grieve and cry out. It's okay to have times of purposelessness and it's okay to be hopeless because what you see ahead is dreary. It's okay to go to a doctor or counselor for depression as a Christian and it's okay to not. It's okay to be sad and hate your circumstances. It's okay to wrestle with the Lord and ask questions. You are unique but your emotions are not. Even Jesus was a man of deep sorrow and grief (Isa. 53:3).

In all things, go to the Father. Remember who He is and who you are in Him. He has called you out of darkness, and now it's time to step into the light full of purpose. You were created for a reason and your pain is not wasted. You're not alone.

Blooming in the Dark

Something Good to Remember: While it doesn't *feel* like God is for us sometimes because of the circumstances He has allowed, God is and will always be for you.

For Reflection: Can you answer each of these questions, honestly, with a resounding *yes*?

Is He good?

Does He love you?

Is He always faithful?

Is He sovereign?

Can you trust Him?

For Meditation: Job 38–39

To Pray: *Thank You, Lord, for being near. Thank You for being my light in a dark world. While I feel out of it, while my heart is heavy, my eyes are clouded and my soul cries out in sorrow, meet me in the dark. Meet me in the places that no one else will. I cry out to You now and ask that You will be with me and renew a steadfast spirit within me. Give me purpose when I see no hope. Amen.*

chapter 11

When You're Forced to Stop: Rest in Christ

"Come to me, all of you who are weary and carry heavy burdens, and I will give you rest."

MATTHEW 11:28

Something Good Will Grow

Circumstances that cause us to stop are blessings in disguise as we learn to truly rest in Christ.

There have been multiple times in my life where I was forced to stop and slow down. It always felt so pointless in the moment.

But seasons of cancer, treatment, and the now daily effects of extreme fatigue have all forced me to stop and learn the blessing of rest. I can now gladly slow down, read a book, or sit on the couch without an ounce of guilt, but it has taken me years to get to this place. I don't do it perfectly, but I have learned how to rest, and I don't ever want to go back to a life without it.

God's Word and slow seasons have taught me the importance of a Sabbath, moments of respite for the soul. Of course, rest is not an excuse to forsake what we are called to do or to withdraw long-term from being a part of a community, but we must find balance. Rest is vital in our walk with Christ to realign our lives to His will.

Throughout this chapter we're going to be talking about how the unfortunate events that cause us to stop are blessings in disguise as we learn the real gift, rest in Christ. Rest is our reward, rest needs to be a rhythm, rest is a realignment toward Christ, and rest is required for a thriving and content life in Christ.

As we touch on each of these, you'll see a thread of God's grace as you learn to breathe in His idea of rest for you and breathe out the unnecessary expectations you may have on yourself. Release those heavy burdens and lay them at the feet of Jesus.

Circumstances that bring your life to an abrupt halt will bring rest for your weary soul when in the hands of God. The Sabbath God's Word describes is as strategic as it is holy.

Rest as a Reward

As I sit down to write this chapter, all the farm animals have been fed, the kitchen is clean, the kids are tucked in bed, the house is picked up, and the dishwasher has been started. Yes, I'm one of those Type A clean freaks who feels like I have to do all those things before I can have "my time" at night. Having everything in order allows me to rest without distraction or, in this case, write without apologizing.

We can call this "planned rest." I get everything in order so that I can have my time. At its core, this is a rest we feel we've earned by successfully controlling the circumstances around us. When I get a moment of planned rest, I'm able to sit and breathe after a long day while watching the sunset through the windows of our master bedroom. This is a rarity!

I think of the story of creation in Genesis 1 and 2 where God rests on the seventh day after creating the whole world in six. He didn't *need* to rest (Acts 17:25). He *chose* to rest. God's day of rest didn't have to be included in the Bible for us to read, but it was. What can we learn from Him? God is setting the standard that after long days of working, creating, cultivating the ground, and breathing life, a day of peace and rest is valuable spiritually, mentally, and physically.

We can look at God and recognize it's okay to reward ourselves in this way. I am following God's example by allowing my body and mind to rest after a long day of managing tasks and serving my family, even though there is *always* more to do. This is when rest is a reward. You put in the work, now you get to rest. It's more of a coordinated rest that you get to implement based on your organized circumstances and productivity. But what if your workload doesn't end until late or your kids aren't in bed yet or you have a sports game to attend or your office called and a project deadline just got moved up?

What happens when you crave your much-deserved rest as your reward for a hard week, but the plates keep spinning and you have to keep going? You see rest slip through the cracks and take the back burner to your unfinished to-do list.

This is when you must take the moments you can. Your rest doesn't get to be planned because life is too much, so you have to actively take the free minutes you might have during your week and offer them up to the Lord so He can recenter you toward His heart.

Rest as a Rhythm

Having health issues that will linger until I meet Jesus has made me learn the value of rest. My entire cancer journey forced me to stop because there was nothing I could do about anything. I had to let everything run its course and, while I felt out of control (because I was) and not in charge (because I'm not), that season of pause was one of the most spiritually fruitful seasons of my life. I hadn't allowed myself to give my mind or body rest before cancer. Resting brought realignment to Christ's will for my life. Implementing rest as a rhythm has made me stronger.

Downtime and rest look different in every season too. I used to be a social butterfly, and recharging was hanging with a few close

The life of Jesus gives us much guidance on the reasons and rhythms of rest.

friends. When I got married, recharging was relaxing at home with my husband. When I had a baby, resting was sleeping whenever I could. Now, as a homeschool mom to four kids, author, speaker, and one taking on homesteading on the farm, rest looks like a few minutes of sitting on the porch. In order to be faithful in all that I do, I have to steal the ten minutes here and there when I can to watch the sunset or read a book. More importantly, I *need* time with the Lord.

I crave alone time now and have to learn to live out a rhythm of rest instead of forcing a planned rest as I rarely can do. Forcing rest just isn't possible as much with my time spread so thin. I'm assuming your life looks the same.

The life of Jesus gives us much guidance on the reasons and rhythms of rest. I love that each of the authors of the gospels made it a specific point to write down the times when Jesus went away to be alone and pray.

- Then Jesus went with them to the olive grove called Gethsemane, and he said, "Sit here while I go over there to pray." (Matt. 26:36)
- Before daybreak the next morning, Jesus got up and went out to an isolated place to pray. (Mark 1:35)
- But Jesus often withdrew to the wilderness for prayer. (Luke 5:16)

While most of Jesus' time wasn't spent alone and in prayer, time with God was essential to His ministry. If Jesus chose time with His Father, how much more do *we* need to choose time with Him?

I need to go to Him more in prayer and be more cognizant of how my time is spent. If we want to live a life that represents the

Lord, we should strive to make our time—all of our time—fruitful. Positive. Peaceful. Fun. Life-giving. Restful. Quiet. Prayerful. Silent. Quality time with people we love. Joy-filled. Honoring. Those can all be glimpses of rest when we allow ourselves, and the people around us, to stop striving.

God wants you and me to enjoy our lives, but when we slow down, would He be watching the TV show you're watching with you? Would God pick up the same book you're reading? Would He be using His time the way you are? And even if the things we are doing are morally neutral, are they really recharging us for the tasks God has assigned to us? Entertainment does not always equal rest; often it drains us rather than refueling us. When rest is scarce but still badly needed, our "yeses" mean saying no to what our minds, bodies, and souls need most.

Sometimes sitting on the porch in the quietness of nature is resting. Sometimes rest for the week might be taking a nap. Maybe your rest is going on a run so that your body and mind feel more at ease and recharged. Maybe rest is taking those moments of prayer that quiet your soul and realign your mind with Christ. Or maybe you just need to sit down, put your phone away, and watch your kids play outside.

Rest is not a to-do list and there is no right or wrong way. One person's resting is different from another's rest, and it doesn't always *look* spiritual to the outsider. And that's okay! The Lord knows your heart.

Cancer taught me that it's possible to glorify God as much when I'm resting as when I'm doing the pattern Jesus modeled. A rhythm of being content in the Lord, at every speed.

When you offer Him up snippets of your time, He will fill you with His grace, comfort, holy refreshment, and peace. That is true rest.

> Then Jesus said, "Come to me, all of you who are weary and carry heavy burdens, and I will give you rest." (Matt. 11:28)

As we go to the Lord first, He will give us what we need and what we've been looking for.

Through Jesus you can experience rest for your soul, no matter what is going on around you. His grace guides you to a kind of rest that makes you feel like you've been lying in green meadows or lingering by peaceful streams (Ps. 23:2). Does this mean an absence of all stress? Of course not. It does mean that when we are weary, we are free to come to Him and experience fulfillment.

Rest as a Realignment

You know when your computer is wonky and you've tried everything to fix it on your own? You restart it, delete old files, close tabs, look through the system preferences, and even ask a friend for help. Then, as the last resort, you decide to shut the whole thing down and for some reason that does the trick. That's how we are. Sometimes the only way for God to get our attention is to have an unseen or sudden occasion that shuts us down, forcing us to gaze into His eyes and craving His plans above our own. What have some of yours been?

I understand David's words in Psalm 119:71 (ESV): "It is good for me that I was afflicted, that I might learn your statutes," and later in verse 75, "I know, O LORD, that your rules are righteous, and that in faithfulness you have afflicted me." I felt powerless at the time, but now I can see that my heart and mind were being recalibrated toward the heart of Jesus. In His faithfulness, I had dreams, goals, and ideas. God gave me purpose for a bright future and hope for what was ahead. In order to heal from cancer, for example, sitting on my bed and barely moving was absolutely required. He replaced my need for control with His rest and in Him, I was not only quieted, but content.

Being realigned to the Lord can feel scary and daunting, but take it from a sister who's been there—it's worth it. Rest is always worth it when the Lord is in control. It might take a while to get used to at first, but learning to rest in Christ is an invaluable lesson.

Rest as a Requirement

Rest is a necessity to a Spirit-led life. How often do you hear the Lord speaking to you when you're rushing around doing a million things? I can't tell you if I've ever heard God speak to me when I'm in the grocery store with my four kids trying my best to get everything on the list, not smashing my cart into strangers, telling the kids not to grab or touch anything, smiling at the passersby, and keeping everyone safe, all while answering the incessant questions of a four-year-old.

It's never happened. Why? Because I am not in a posture of receiving in moments like those, but also because I'm not giving the Lord space to speak in a situation like that. Could He? Absolutely, but those are the times where life is happening and things have to get done. There is grace for that!

> *If you want to grow spiritually, pray for and create more moments of rest in your life.*

But slowing down is sacred because it's the moments of rest that you finally offer up your time (the thing we value most!) and God replenishes it with His grace. His voice. His truth. His peace.

I sure don't want to be a woman too busy for Jesus. I've shared this before, but moving to The Faithful Homestead has dramatically shaped our value of time and rest. Because I was always in the car driving kids to school and sports and doing all the things, it was harder for me to find those moments of quiet.

Life was loud and full, but not necessarily life-giving and never slow. Now I bask in His creation like never before and treasure my time with Him because I know rest in Him is my lifeline. I cannot go a day without moments with my Savior. It doesn't look the same every day, and that's okay! It's just about offering the Lord what you can, prioritizing Him, and then watching His grace pour out.

If you want to grow spiritually, pray for and create more moments of rest in your life. Rest is absolutely required for your healing, especially as women who have walked through a lot of pain and suffering in life. That's something I didn't know for years because I thought staying busy would help me heal and get through the trials. I wanted to stay occupied and shove my pain down. But when you sit in the uncomfortable silence and you offer up your time and attention to the Lord, His grace will wash over you all the more as He mends your broken heart and restores what you lost. It's a promise!

> "For I have given rest to the weary and joy to the sorrowing." (Jer. 31:25)

Until you see the value of rest, you will spend your entire life exalting your work and elevating your achievements, never realizing the secret to success all along has been His presence. It's never been about what you do or create in this life. It's always been about knowing your Creator, the One who delights in you.

Ask yourself:

- Am I so busy proving myself that I have forgotten that Jesus is my only source of true peace?
- Are there things I can cut out of my to-do list to make more time with Jesus?
- Is my free time honoring and life-giving?

Those questions are as uncomfortable for me as they likely are for you. Unfortunately, our results-oriented culture is obsessed with doing and neglects resting. I used to pride myself on all that I did for Jesus, but was completely wrecked and humbled by various major challenges, which ultimately showed me His presence is worth more than anything I could possibly achieve or do for Him.

The secret to success all along has been His presence.

Rest brings the healing. Rest brings the hearing. Rest brings the humility because time with Jesus doesn't leave you unchanged or chained to your old ways. Rest frees you, restores you, and deepens your faith and trust in God.

Actively Rest

I know rest can be difficult to consistently prioritize, but don't feel like a failure. There is grace for us when we get it wrong . . .

- when you've put our work or accomplishments or to-do list above time with Jesus,
- when you thought God would be prouder of you for your works for Him instead of being washed with His grace,
- when you've avoided time with God because you were afraid of the outcome,
- when your pride gets in the way,
- when you're mindless or lazy with the time you have been given . . .

Jesus' invitation in Matthew 11:28 remains: "Come to me, all of you who are weary and carry heavy burdens, and I will give you rest."

Let's remember that Sundays are not our only Sabbath or else we could just check it off like any other works-based accomplishment. Sabbath is about your heart motives, giving your mind, body, and soul the space to receive from the Lord and realign your will to His. That's sacred rest. Church can be busy and wild with kids and serving and rushing between services, so don't be so quick to check "church" off your list and think you've had your fill of rest in Christ.

I'm sure someone is thinking right about now, "But I don't have the time to rest!" I know we all have full plates. It's rare to meet someone with a blank slate of a week. But let's be women who actively rest in God's presence. Lean into the seasons when we are forced to stop. The more we quiet ourselves in rest, the more we make ourselves available to hear from the Lord, and the more we begin to heal. The world needs more healed and listening women abiding in Christ! Invite Him into the chaos of your life. Reclaim those small moments throughout the day for Him.

Remember Jesus' friends Mary and Martha? Jesus and His disciples came to their home, and Martha became distracted by the preparations for the meal for a crowd. But Mary chose to sit at Jesus' feet and listen to His teaching. You and I understand Martha's annoyance. When she asked Jesus to send Mary into the kitchen to help her, He said, "My dear Martha, you are worried and upset over all these details! There is only one thing worth being concerned about. Mary has discovered it, and it will not be taken away from her" (Luke 10:41–42).

Choose Christ and rest in Him. We're all doing our best. I can't tell you how important it has been for me as a mom with health challenges to do this. He gives me Himself when I pause and offer Him what I can. His grace will cover your busy days and your endless to-do lists. His words will strengthen you and His voice will speak directly to your needs. Let's be women who are quick to rest and sit at His feet today.

Here are some practical ideas for rest. I pray they spark your journey to rest as you receive His grace in return.

- While you're washing dishes or doing laundry, put in headphones or crank up instrumental worship music.
- Close your closet door in the middle of the chaos and sit in silence for five minutes. Everyone will be okay.
- Wake up early to spend time with the Lord.

- Go for a walk, or somewhere alone on your lunch break.
- Be quick to say no so that your schedule isn't so full. Your spiritual health is more important than people's opinions.
- If you stay home with your kids, enforce a daily quiet time for everyone.
- Prayerfully consider deleting an app that takes too much of your time.
- Get out in nature when you can.

Blooming in the Dark

Something Good to Remember: Slowing down is sacred because it's in the moments of rest that you finally offer up your time (the thing we value most!) and God replaces it with His grace.

For Reflection: If you are resistant to rest, what do you think is truly driving that resistance?

For Meditation: Jeremiah 31:25

To Pray: *Father God, I am learning to rest in You but still have such a difficult time finding moments alone. With everything on my plate, will You open up my schedule so that I can take even five minutes of solitude with You? You are my treasure, so take my time and rest as an offering. Thank You for pouring out Your wisdom and grace even when life is heavy. I love You, Lord.*

in closing

Broken Up Soil in God's Faithful Hands

There's a reason the psalmist never sang about the beauty of brown pastures.

On one area of our farm, a pasture, once green and lush, turned into a field of brownish red dirt, hard as a rock. Over time, with all the rain and animals and weather and usage, it was no longer producing green grass in the spring. Instead, it was barren and fruitless.

We had to break it apart. We had to dig it up, put the cows in another pasture, let the soil rest, put a certain fertilizer on it, and then give it more time. I've seen it with my own eyes: Broken up soil in the hands of a faithful God produces good fruit.

With time and effort, and a lot of patience, the pasture finally became green and lush again. If we'd just left it? Season after season? That field would have never changed. The dry, fruitlessness would have gotten worse, then spread. Producing nothing, growing nothing, and honestly just a muddy mess in the winter and an ant's favorite place to build in the summer.

Now we are reaping the benefits of hard work and labor. Cows can eat its fresh green blades, kids can play in it, and it's beautiful to look at.

Moving On from a Muddy Mess

I know we don't like the idea that good fruit, like godly character, perseverance, hope, strength, and beauty are produced from broken up soil. Soil that's been watered and molded and crafted by the hands of God, who alone can produce miracles out of dirt. We'd rather just get through life, keeping pain at a distance, never fully investing in people and our purpose because of the fears of suffering that hold us back. We'd rather be untouched by His good and perfect plans if it means we have to face pain or worse, persecution or devastation.

Our heart's cry becomes "don't work on me, Lord. I don't want to surrender because it's too hard. Let me be."

Ultimately, many of us would rather remain a muddy mess in the winter and a place for ant piles in the summer. Without ever verbalizing it, our heart's cry becomes "don't work on me, Lord. I don't want to surrender because it's too hard. Let me be." We want to coast through life, never fully surrendered, never fully thriving, never fully blooming.

I understand this feeling and I think most of us could admit that we struggle to want to be molded, crafted, broken, or uprooted, because all of that is *painful.* It's hard. It's uncomfortable. We'd rather not deal with what comes from going from point A to point B. We'd rather just sit on A forever even if it means we won't fully experience His abundant goodness and gifts and glory.

But is that what we want, *really?* Our souls long to be green pastures, fertilized and flourishing, not muddy pits where nothing good can grow.

Is your fear of pain keeping the good from growing in you?

God graciously wants you and I to see that with Him, our suffering has purpose. When He is the King of our life, He can work miracles out of devastation. Read how Augustine of Hippo (AD 354–430), an early church leader and theologian, explained this. His descriptive words are relevant all these years later:

> When the good and the wicked suffer alike, the identity of their sufferings does not mean that there is no difference between them. Though the sufferings are the same, the sufferers remain different. Virtue and vice are not the same, even if they undergo the same torment. The fire which makes gold shine makes chaff smoke; the same flail breaks up the straw, and clears the grain; and oil is not mistaken for less because both are forced out by the same press. In the same way, the violence which assails good men to test them, to cleanse and purify them, effects in the wicked their condemnation, ruin, and annihilation. Thus the wicked, under pressure of affliction, execrate God and blaspheme; the good, in the same affliction, offer up prayers and praises. This shows that what matters is the nature of the sufferer, not the nature of the sufferings. Stir a cesspit, and a foul stench arises; stir a perfume, and a delightful fragrance ascends. But the movement is identical.[10]

Because of Christ, the nature of your suffering can look hope-filled and purposeful in the hands of the God who loves you. We *all* have suffering. It's so important to remember this because it's not a contest of who goes through what in this life and who has the crazier, most profound testimony (we all have a testimony!). *What matters is the surrender of the sufferer, not the details of the sufferings.* How do you walk through trials? How do you react? What are your questions? Do you remain faithful? Do you cling to Christ or do you run? Not that the particulars of sufferings don't matter, but *you* matter more. How you're refined and shaped for His glory matters.

Brokenness as Our Sacrifice

In the Old Testament, God's people were instructed to make sacrifices to atone for their sin. For example, when people became aware of their sin, they would bring a bull to the tabernacle as an offering for their sin, and the "elders of the community" would slaughter it. Then the high priest would take the blood into the tabernacle, dip his finger in the blood, and sprinkle it seven times before the Lord in front of the inner curtain (Lev. 4:15, 17). The details continue as the remaining blood has specifications on how it is supposed to be used so their sins would be washed away from them.

These sacrifices had to be repeated over and over. All this is because "without the shedding of blood, there is no forgiveness" (Heb. 9:22) of sin.

But then God sent His Son, Jesus Christ, as the ultimate sacrifice for our sins. "God made Christ, who never sinned, to be the offering for our sin, so that we could be made right with God" (2 Cor. 5:21). His blood that was shed on the cross was the perfect sacrifice for our sins now, forever and always. What a gift! While God's people don't need to ever again sacrifice animals in order to get right with Him, we are still called to a deep dependence on the Lord and deep contrition before Him. We must be affected by our sin, broken by our sin, and understand our spiritual poverty that separates us from God. That is our sacrifice today.

When you give Him your pain and allow Him to work in your life in spite of trials and suffering, you are offering the most pleasing of sacrifices.

Psalm 51:17 beautifully says to the Lord, "The sacrifice you desire is a broken spirit. You will not reject a broken and repentant heart, O God." The psalmist is saying that the sacrifice we must offer the Lord is not a broken or slaughtered animal anymore, but a broken heart. And if you're reading this, you and I, my friend, have broken hearts. After all that we have walked through, we have a deep understanding that we are but dust without our Savior. But with Him, we are whole and set apart!

The suffering we have walked, are walking through, and will walk through can either negatively define the rest of our days, or become the most beautiful sacrifice we can offer the Lord. God is "close to the brokenhearted" (Ps. 34:18), and when you give Him your pain and allow Him to work in your life in spite of trials and suffering, you are offering the most pleasing of sacrifices. Let's bring Him great praise and honor for healing us through our brokenness.

Something Good Will Grow

What I hope this book has shown you is that it is a privilege to suffer with and for Christ. Don't take my word for it. Listen again to Paul's words recorded in Philippians 1:29.

> For you have been given not only the privilege of trusting in Christ but also the privilege of suffering for him.

Suffering is a privilege, not because we like pain and trials, but because we know that God cares so much about our sanctification, that out of His great love for us, He uses our trials for our good and His glory. He allows our worst times and darkest days to produce character, to grow perseverance, and to keep our eyes on the hope and joy of our salvation so that we can live in abundance here and now.

I never want to walk through tribulations, but because of mine, God has greatly blessed me. Consider this: "It is doubtful whether God can bless a man greatly until he has hurt him deeply."[11]

When I heard this quote by A. W. Tozer in a sermon many years ago, it honestly shocked me. *That's not true*, I thought. I immediately wanted to defend the kind character of God and smash the idea that God hurts us. But as I wrestled with it more and more, I realized how true it is.

Maybe the question becomes, *Can God's rich blessings and our lifelong sanctification happen without the hurt and pain of life?*

You see, at first, I applied this quote to my own life: rape and cancer and losing a baby and so on and thought how wrong it was to think that God had to hurt me in those ways in order to bless me. That's messed-up thinking because God loves us! He takes no pleasure in our pain. This is why statements like "everything happens for a reason" can be so damaging, because while God knows and sees all, He doesn't orchestrate evil. He uses the promised evil we'll face for our good.

But I had the meaning backward. Once I understood more clearly, Tozer's words reminded me of being purified by *fire*. Hurt, suffering, pain, trials. We all want to be the shiny pearl or the glistening diamond or the beautiful piece of pottery in the end, but we don't want to go through what it takes to get us there.

Tozer continued: "We overlook the place of the thorns, the cross, and the blood. We ignore the function of the hammer and the file."[12]

He meant that the pain of the thorns that pierced our Lord, the cross where He was nailed, and the blood that was shed as a sacrifice for all humankind cannot go unnoticed. *It was through the trenches of utter darkness and evil that hope was birthed.*

God loves you so much that He's using the evil you have personally come face-to-face with to sanctify you so that you *don't* remain a dull, rough-edged piece of rock. Instead, when you surrender your life into the hands of Almighty God, He chisels and spins and molds you into a shining diamond or piece of art that can only give credit to its Craftsman. And that process hurts. And because God is good and sovereign, *He greatly blesses us through the hurt He allows.* This gives us so much hope.

We can now have hope in the health challenges.

Hope in the chaos.

Hope in the depression and loneliness.

Hope in the storms.

Hope in the messed-up plans.

Hope in the insecurities and the exhaustion.

Hope in the waiting and difficult relationships.

You can too. The something good that grows in us through trials is real, unshakable hope and a better understanding of God's heart for us in the middle of pain. I love how Romans 5:5 says it: "And this hope will not lead to disappointment. For we know how dearly God loves us, because he has given us the Holy Spirit to fill our hearts with his love."

Hope that doesn't disappoint . . . that's what is forged in us through the fires of life. What a beautiful, priceless treasure that is!

> The trials God allows on earth are stepping stones to becoming more like Christ and growing in His Word

The goal of my life is to be made more like Christ and glorify the Lord all of my days. I want to know Him and sit at a table with all the saints and martyrs and men and women of faith who have gone before me. I want to talk with the humble and the faithful, nameless on earth, but with a crown full of jewels in heaven. Those who were unseen, blooming in the dark, but did great things for the Lord. I want to be among the women who fought for their families, for their healing, for their generation, knowing full well that the trials God allowed on earth were stepping stones to becoming more like Christ and growing in His Word.

If I've learned anything, it's that the refining has a purpose. The brokenness has a purpose. The growing pains have a purpose. The darkness has a purpose. The uncomfortable sifting has a purpose. And all of it hurts. But Jesus understands. It was His greatest trial, death on the cross, that brought the greatest reward, life abundant. His trial was our triumph. His pain bought our redemption. His brokenness ushered in beauty. When you finally surrender to Christ and understand what He has for you and what He has done for you, you rest in a peaceful hope, knowing even in this hard place and mess, you are blooming for His glory.

As you close this book, I pray you see God's heart in the soil of your suffering and always remember that something good is growing.

> *We can rejoice, too, when we run into problems and trials, for we know that they help us develop endurance. And endurance develops strength of character, and character strengthens our confident hope of salvation. And this hope will not lead to disappointment. For we know how dearly God loves us, because he has given us the Holy Spirit to fill our hearts with his love.* Romans 5:3–5

Doxology

Now to him who is able to keep you from stumbling and to present you blameless before the presence of his glory with great joy, to the only God, our Savior, through Jesus Christ our Lord, be glory, majesty, dominion, and authority, before all time and now and forever. Amen.

JUDE 24–25 ESV

Acknowledgments

Thank you to the entire Moody Publishers team for not only believing in me and being the bridge to a redemptive story in my life, but for making this message what it is today. I am honored to work with you and am so grateful for your talent, time, and wisdom.

Thank you to Erin for always having my back and challenging me in the best ways.

Thank you to Rick for your wise counsel as you helped me piece parts of myself back together.

Thank you to the women on our prayer team—for your support, diligent intercession, and willingness to serve.

To my Community Bible Study group—your insight, prayers, and encouragement carried me through this season.

Thank you to my best friends who endlessly listen and pray, keep me accountable, and always push me to Christ, through all of the highs and lows. I couldn't do life without any of you.

To my four children—my greatest joys. Thank you for giving me the time and grace to write these words. You are the most incredible kids in the world and I love being your mom!

Thank you to Andrew—you are my biggest blessing, my favorite person, and I'd never be here without your unconditional love, your steady character, and your relentless truth.

Lastly, and most importantly, thank You, Lord, for giving a broken person like me an opportunity to share about Your faithfulness with others. I don't take it lightly and pray this book would be an offering to You.

All for Your glory.

Notes

1. © 1996–present, *The Enduring Word Bible Commentary* by David Guzik, https://enduringword.com/bible-commentary/2-corinthians-1.
2. Oswald Chambers, *My Utmost for His Highest* (Discovery House Publishers, 1992), January 6 selection.
3. © 1996–present, *The Enduring Word Bible Commentary* by David Guzik, https://enduringword.com/bible-commentary/nehemiah-9.
4. Mark Vroegop, *Dark Clouds, Deep Mercy: Discovering the Grace of Lament* (Crossway, 2019), 77.
5. A. W. Tozer, *The Root of the Righteous* (Moody Publishers, 2015), 103.
6. C. H. Spurgeon, *All of Grace: An Earnest Word for Those Who are Seeking Salvation by the Lord Jesus Christ* (Moody Publishers, 2010), 32.
7. Helen M. Roseveare, *Living Sacrifice: Willing to Be Whittled as an Arrow* (Christian Focus Publications, 2007), 113.
8. A. W. Tozer, *The Root of the Righteous* (Moody Publishers, 2015), 151.
9. Proverbs 12:25 is quoted from the New King James Version® of the Bible. Copyright © 1982 by Thomas Nelson.
10. Saint Augustine, *Concerning the City of God against the Pagans* (Penguin Books, 2003), 14.
11. A. W. Tozer, *The Root of the Righteous* (Moody Publishers, 2015), 165.
12. Tozer, *The Root of the Righteous*, 166.